1974

THE PUNT PASS AND KICK
NFL
LIBRARY

DISCA

Great Linebackers of the NFL

The biographical sketches of ten great linebackers, past and present, of the National Football League. The players range from Mel Hein and "Bulldog" Turner, who starred in the days of two-way players, to the current linebacking heroes of platoon football—Dick Butkus, Tommy Nobis, Wayne Walker, Dave Robinson, Mike Curtis, Ray Nitschke, Chuck Howley, and Maxie Baughan.

GREAT LINEBACKERS
of the NFL

by RICHARD KAPLAN

Illustrated with photographs

RANDOM HOUSE
NEW YORK

This title was originally catalogued by the Library of Congress as follows:

Kaplan, Richard.
 Great linebackers of the NFL. New York, Random House
 [1970]

  vii, 144 p. illus., ports. 22 cm. (The Punt, pass, and kick library,
12)

  Highlights the football careers of ten National Football League
linebackers of past and present: Butkus, Hein, Turner, Nitschke,
Baughan, Walker, Robinson, Howley, Curtis, and Nobis.

  1. Football—Biography—Juvenile literature. [1. Football—Biog-
raphy] 2. National Football League. I. Title.

GV939.A1K3   70–90291

                          796.332′0922 [920]
                                                            MARC
    Library of Congress   70 [4]   A C

Trade Ed.: ISBN: 0-394-80152-0   Lib. Ed.: ISBN: 0-394-90152-5

© Copyright, 1970, by Random House, Inc.

Manufactured in the United States of America

Photograph Credits: John Biever: 93; Vernon J. Biever: front endpaper, viii, 12–13, 42, 47, 52, 86, 97, 125, 128; Dallas Cowboys: 100;
Detroit Lions—George Gellatly: 70, 84; Malcolm W. Emmons: 112,
114, 117, 122; Emmons and Brockway: 8; New York Daily News: 16;
Darryl Norenberg—Camera 5: 62, 64, 77; Ken Regan—Camera 5:
back endpaper; 74–75, 135; United Press International: ii, 4, 11, 24,
29, 30, 36–37, 44, 54–55, 58, 90, 104, 109, 131; Wide World Photos:
139.

Cover photo (Dick Butkus): By Malcolm Emmons

Contents

Introduction

Defensive football players come in three distinctive varieties. Linemen are huge men with awesome strength. Backs must be fast enough to cover receivers with Olympic sprinter speed. And then there are the linebackers, who have to combine all the assets of linemen and backs. Linebackers must be fast, big, *and* tough. It is not true that the linebacker is the most important position in professional football; quarterback is. But on defense, there's no question that the linebackers play the key role.

The position of linebacker is not new. The linebacker has had an important job in pro football for more than a generation—as the stories in this book on Mel Hein and Bulldog Turner demonstrate. They starred as NFL linebackers in the 1930s and 1940s. But linebacking did not really sink into the popular consciousness until the 1950s, when an important offensive change forced a defensive reaction. The offense introduced a third end, called the slot back.

The pros had been playing a 5-4-2 defense (five linemen, four linebackers, two safeties). But the "5-4," as the pros called it, became obsolete with the advent of the slot back. A new 4-3-2-2 defense (four linemen, three linebackers, two cornerbacks, two safeties) came into vogue. The new linebackers had to be both big and fast. They had to be able to charge into the line to get the quarterback or stop runners, but they also had to be able to roam the field with the opponent's pass receivers, when the situation called for it.

The new era was typified by such linebackers as Sam Huff of the New York Giants and Joe Schmidt of the Detroit Lions, both of whom have been chronicled in detail in a previous Punt, Pass & Kick Library book, *Great Defensive Players of the NFL*. Since the emergence of Huff and Schmidt, linebacking has become one of the most popular positions in pro football. Thus, the exploits of ten of the finest linebackers are collected and told in this new book—*Great Linebackers of the NFL*.

DICK BUTKUS

There comes a moment of truth for every first-year pro football player, especially for one who carries an All-America reputation. In the case of Dick Butkus, that moment of truth came very, very early. In the 1965 College All-Star Game against the National Football League champion Cleveland Browns, Butkus, the defensive captain of the All-Stars, was stationed at his customary middle linebacker post when he saw what for him was a most uncustomary sight. Through a big hole in the collegians' defensive line surged Cleveland's 228-pound fullback, Jim Brown, perhaps the greatest runner professional football has seen or ever will see. Legs churning, shoulders lowered, Brown bore down on Butkus like a rhinoceros.

Butkus reacted swiftly and instinctively. A big man at 245 pounds, he hurled himself fearlessly into the onrushing Brown. The collision was crushing as muscle met muscle. Strong men were known to bounce off Jim Brown like BB gun pellets—but not Dick Butkus. He dropped the famous Cleveland power runner in his tracks. Both men got up slowly. It was as if the All-Pro fullback had said, "Welcome to pro football," and the powerful young collegiate linebacker had replied, "It's nice to be here."

Dick Butkus. Even the name sounds tough. And during his first five seasons with the Chicago Bears, the man that name belongs to developed into one of the NFL's classic linebackers. As a matter of fact, Butkus became a legend in his rookie season.

First, however, there was the little matter of winning a starting job with the Bears. Butkus got his chance when age and a bad knee finally slowed down the Bears' All-League middle linebacker, Bill George. The Chicago coaches decided to start Butkus at George's old position and let the rookie learn by his mistakes. They were confident that he would be making fewer and fewer errors as the 1965 season wore on.

Butkus progressed faster than anyone had expected. Not even his coaches could have predicted that by the end of the year he would be voted All-NFL at middle linebacker—an amazing achievement for a newcomer playing the most demanding position on defense. Butkus also would have been Rookie of the Year had it not been for his super-spectacular teammate, halfback Gale Sayers. Backs usually get the glory.

Butkus' rise to All-NFL prominence sounds so easy, but of course it was not. Behind that almost instant success in pro ball stretched a lifetime of desire and effort.

"There's only one thing I've ever wanted to do," said Butkus. "Play pro football. Everyone seems to be made for something. I've always felt that playing pro football was the thing I was supposed to do."

In that first year, Butkus received what amounted to a crash course in linebacking. Although it helps, brute force is never enough in the NFL. Smart application of brute force is what counts—and what many players find so difficult to learn. Butkus had been well coached at the University of Illinois, where he had played middle linebacker each of his three varsity seasons. And there was never any question about his willingness and ability to hit. Butkus is perhaps the most physical football player playing today. He thrives on body contact. But a middle linebacker must know more than how to hit, particularly when he is the hub of a defense as intricate as the one employed by the Bears.

The Chicago team confuses opponents with a wide variety of stunts and blitzing patterns. But the system can confuse a Bear rookie, too. Butkus had to learn to protect his territory instead of deserting it to make a tackle.

"In college," Dick explained, "I used to just sort of free-lance. I would go anywhere I wanted to. But in pro ball a middle linebacker has a responsibility to protect a certain territory. Like in pass coverage. You cover your man first of all. Then, if somebody starts to run with the ball, you go tackle him. But it's dangerous to be too eager. If too many guys try to do more than their job, you get hurt."

From his very first game Butkus knew how much he had to learn. Against the San Francisco Forty-Niners the Bears gave up tremendous yardage on draw plays up the middle. Although Dick made eleven tackles during the afternoon, it looked as if the Forty-Niners had been able to lure him out of position too often. But when Coach George Halas looked at the game films, he cleared Butkus of blame. "Dick was never seriously trapped," Halas said. "He was doing his assigned job—blast and hit. That's what he does best."

As the season went on, Butkus blasted and hit better and better. He had excellent teachers in George Allen, then the Chicago defensive coach, and his fellow linebackers, veterans Joe Fortunato, Larry Morris and Bill George.

When the Bears played the Baltimore Colts, Butkus recovered four Colt fumbles and intercepted two passes as Chicago beat Baltimore, 13-0. It was the first time the Colts had been shut out in forty-three regular-season games. George Allen couldn't hide his delight. "I don't know how much more improvement is possible," he said, "but Dick just gets better and better every game. He's already doing things you'd expect only from a fellow with a couple years' experience. This boy is all football player—this is Number One with him. He's determined to be the best there is. He

Butkus, blocking a Johnny Unitas pass,
made the All-Pro team as a rookie.

has great football sense and he gives you that extra effort all the time. You ask a football player for one hundred per cent. This boy gives you one hundred and ten per cent all the time."

The opposition was equally impressed. Said Baltimore coach Don Shula, "Butkus is so strong he can tackle the runner and search him for the ball at the same time."

Later that year, the Bears played the Forty-Niners again. This time Butkus stopped the San Francisco draw play cold. He helped hold the Forty-Niners to only 58 yards rushing and the San Francisco fullback, Ken Willard, gained a mere 24 yards.

When asked to analyze what he had learned during his rookie season, Butkus said, "Every game I play now I learn more about how to counter the opposition's attack. Before, I played it the same way, whether it was first-and-twenty or fourth-and-one. Now I know there are other things to consider, like the down and distance, field position, being a policeman for the team, and being in the right place at the right time."

More important, these things were rapidly becoming almost reflex reactions. They have to be, because as Butkus himself put it, "One thing I'm sure of is that you can't think too much out there. If you do, it's too late to do anything. If you take time to think, you're dead."

Ever since a writer for a national magazine wrote a snide article about Butkus during Dick's senior year at Illinois, the big fellow has had to overcome the reputation of being all brawn and no brains. Butkus admits that he is no Phi Beta Kappa, but he resents the implication that he is some kind of muscular oaf. Chuck Bednarik, the former Philadelphia Eagle linebacker, said the charge that Butkus is "dumb" is ridiculous.

"Chicago has by far the most complicated defensive system in the league," said Bednarik, "and that guy Butkus runs it. Anybody who does that has got to be intelligent. And George Halas wouldn't give Butkus the responsibility if he didn't know that Dick would do the job. From watching Butkus play, I'd say that he is an extremely intelligent football player."

Bill George, the man Butkus replaced, agreed with Bednarik. "I think Butkus has gotten a bum rap," George said. "Dick calls the plays out there. He's an intelligent, inspiring ballplayer."

Before the 1969 season Butkus may have improved his intellectual image by turning to the study of the works of William Shakespeare. "I've found that reading Shakespeare aloud improves my diction and enunciation," Dick said, "and I think it may help me as a football player. Take this situation: one of our men is shaken up on a play and is slow getting up. The opposing blocker is standing over him laughing. I walk over and instead of snarling at the guy, maybe starting a fight and getting thrown out of the game, I just tell him: 'He jests at scars that never felt a wound.' Now that is bound to set him thinking and teach him a little humility."

No one, of course, has questioned Butkus' ability to make speedy decisions on the football field. However, his leg speed has been under scrutiny, especially in comparison to his middle linebacking rivals of the 1960s—Tommy Nobis and Ray Nitschke. But Bill George has spoken in Dick's defense in this regard, too.

"They [the critics] always complain about Butkus' speed," George said in 1968, "but Dick seldom gets beat. I can't agree with anybody who says he isn't fast enough. He gets the job done, regardless of how fast he can run the hundred. And that's what counts."

Actually combining his super sense of what is going on with what speed he has, Butkus stuns opponents with some of his plays. The New York Giants found that out in a game against the Bears in 1969. On a last-minute swing pass to Giant halfback Joe Morrison, the Chicago corner linebacker assigned to cover Morrison was faked out of position. It looked as if Morrison could walk right down the field to the end zone for the go-ahead touchdown. When Morrison caught the pass, Butkus was in the middle of the field, yards and yards away. Somehow Dick sensed what was going to happen and headed for Morrison. The New York halfback barely made it over the goal line as the onrushing Butkus bowled him over.

Quarterback Fran Tarkenton of the Giants,

Dick has the ability to find out which way the play is going—and the ability to track down his man.

who had thrown the pass, was astounded at Butkus' movement. "As I watched the play develop,"
Tarkenton said, "I was sure we had an easy touchdown if I could just get the ball to Morrison. But
Butkus almost pulled it out for the Bears. He's
something else. You better believe it."

The statistics bear out George's and Tarkenton's analysis. As a rookie, Butkus led the Bears in
interceptions with five, and he is no longer re-
garded as a soft touch on passing plays. He has
learned to read keys shrewdly and, as he showed
against the Giants, gains that extra step by sheer
anticipation. Undeniably, however, Dick is
tougher against running plays, where his awesome
ability to sniff out the play, plow though the
blockers and get to the ball-carrier are unsur-
passed.

Dick Butkus, it seems, was born to play football. Dick was raised in Chicago, one of eight
children in a Lithuanian-American family. He
began playing football in grammar school, when
he was in the eighth grade. At that time he played
fullback and linebacker.

Butkus could have gone to a high school close
to home, but he chose Chicago Vocational High
School, which was about a twenty-minute ride
away. Why Chicago Vocational? Because the
school had a good football coach, Bernie O'Brien,
who had played for Notre Dame. Butkus had
heard about O'Brien and wanted to play for him.
With Dick in the lineup, Chicago Vocational was
public school champion twice and city co-

champion once. He made the all-state team as a fullback.

Naturally, the college recruiters clustered around Butkus, who was considered one of the nation's blue-chip schoolboy prospects. Dick considered Notre Dame and a few Big Ten colleges, then chose Illinois. Head Coach Pete Elliott was delighted. "Without question," recalled Elliott, "we knew from the day Dick reported that he was a great one. He moved well and he had a sure instinct to do the right things. I never saw him take a loafing step." Elliott made the comment that Butkus would someday win the Heisman Trophy, an honor usually reserved for backs.

As a sophomore, Butkus made ninety-seven tackles in seven games. As a junior, he made 145

At Illinois, Dick helped Coach
Pete Elliott win the Rose Bowl.

tackles in ten games. As a senior it was 132 tackles in nine games. In 1963, his junior year, Butkus led Illinois to the Big Ten championship and victory in the Rose Bowl. He made All-America that season and again in 1964, when he was also named Lineman of the Year. Although he finished third in the voting for the Heisman Trophy, behind backs John Huarte of Notre Dame and Tucker Frederickson of Auburn, Butkus has outstripped both of them in the pros.

Just as the colleges had competed for Butkus, so did the pro football leagues. The era of the big-money war between the leagues was in progress. Butkus was a first-round draft choice of both the NFL Chicago Bears and the AFL Denver Broncos. Through his attorney, Butkus played it cagey, but there was little doubt where he wanted to play—provided the price was right. Chicago was his hometown. The Bears were his team. The NFL was his league.

On December 3, 1964, Butkus signed a contract with the Bears that reportedly added up to about $200,000. At that time it was the most money ever paid to a defensive player. George Halas said that Butkus would be used at middle linebacker, but might also make an outstanding offensive center since he had played that position at Illinois, too.

The fat contract did not swell Butkus' head. But the rest of his body ballooned. Before long his weight had risen from 245 to 260 pounds, and

Dick pulls down Green Bay's Donny Anderson.

there was talk that he might eat his way out of being a linebacker and wind up playing defensive end or tackle.

Then Coach Halas intervened. As usual, "Papa Bear" took no nonsense. "Dick," he said, "you can be a pretty good linebacker at 260 pounds. You can be a very good one at 250. But to be a great one, you'll need that extra step, which means you'll have to weigh no more than 245."

That was all Butkus had to hear. He reported to the College All-Star camp at a trim 245. He played brilliantly against the world champion Cleveland Browns, making or helping to make fifteen tackles, then moved directly into the Bears' starting lineup. He has been there ever since—a perennial Pro Bowl selection, always among the top two or three middle linebackers in the NFL. In 1969 he was everyone's All-Pro selection—a black-jerseyed apparition with that big Number 51 staring in the quarterback's face.

Dick Butkus. Quarterbacks and running backs alike know the name well. And they fear the sound of it.

MEL HEIN

Who was the greatest linebacker in the history of the New York Giants? If someone told you it was a name with four letters, beginning with "H," you might answer "Huff," for Sam Huff. That would be close—but wrong. Huff, the Giants' famous middle linebacker of the mid-1950s and early 1960s, was certainly an outstanding player at his position. More than anybody else, Sam helped bring recognition and glamor to defensive players. But Sam Huff wasn't the greatest Giant linebacker of them all. That honor belongs to Mel Hein, the 225-pound iron man who started every game but one during his fifteen-year career with the Giants. Hein made the All-NFL team eight straight years, won the league's Most Valuable Player award once, and was voted a charter member of the National Professional Football Hall of Fame in Canton, Ohio.

Though precise records were not kept when Hein starred, he is believed to have logged more playing time than any other player in the history of the NFL. Mel played from 1931 to 1945, the era of one-platoon football. Most of the time, he played sixty bruising minutes, offense and defense, Sunday after Sunday after Sunday. On offense, Hein played center. On defense, he was a linebacker—and it's as a linebacker that he wants to be remembered.

"I made my name backing up the line," he said proudly. "I made it bumping into some pretty tough people. Anyway, who ever remembers an offensive center?"

When Mel Hein joined the Giants in 1931, pro defenses looked a lot different than they do today. The Giants used a simple 6-2 defensive alignment, with two linebackers. Hein was stationed at right linebacker. As Mel recalled, linebacking wasn't as difficult then as it is in modern football. "Every team used the single-wing offense," he said, "and single-wing plays took longer to develop. You could see them coming. So the linebackers had more time in which to react, to make their moves. We didn't have as many responsibilities as linebackers do today. I had to watch out for wide plays, to make sure the runner didn't get outside me, and I had to take the first man out of the backfield on my side if it looked like a pass play. But we saw a lot more running than passing in those days."

Later in Hein's career, Coach Steve Owen of the Giants made a daring move. He was the first to employ the 5-3-3 defense, utilizing three linebackers. Owen made this move in an attempt to counter the T formation, which sent backs shooting through the line so rapidly that an extra linebacker was needed to cope with them. Hein played right linebacker in the Giants' 5-3. Did linebackers blitz in those days? According to Hein they did, but they never used terms like blitz or "red dog." Their only concession to fancy terminology was to call this maneuver "stunting."

Looking back, Mel feels that only the kindness of a local postmaster made him a New York Giant. Born in Redding, California, on August 22, 1909, Mel and his family moved to Washington when he was a boy. He played high school football, first at Bellingham High School and subsequently at Burlington High. Even then he was a center-linebacker. In his junior year at Burlington, however, he played halfback—and not too well. "I was too big and too gangly," Hein recalled. "I just wasn't comfortable back there."

Hein went to college at Washington State. As a senior, he made the All-America team and led State into the Rose Bowl against Alabama on New Year's Day of 1931. "They passed us silly," Mel recalled. "We had just never seen that kind of passing. We just couldn't stop their long pass plays." Alabama won, 24-0.

There was no such thing as a draft of college players at that time. The pro teams simply contacted the college players they wanted to sign, and it was up to the player to decide which offer to accept. Hein received offers from both the Portsmouth (Virginia) Spartans and the Providence (Rhode Island) Steamrollers. Both were NFL franchises. He also got letters expressing interest from the Giants and the Chicago Bears. But neither team extended a contract or made a firm salary offer. Providence did. The Steamrollers offered to pay Hein $135 a game. Mel considered the contract carefully. He had not attended Washington State on a scholarship, and during his four years he had fallen $1,000 into debt. Moreover, he wanted to get married. If he didn't play pro football, what would he do? Hein looked around. He found that high school football coaches in Washington were earning from $1,000 to $1,700 a year. At that rate, Mel would need several years to pay off his debts. If he accepted the Providence offer, he would earn about $1,800, and he could supplement his income with an off-season job.

Hein's college coaches did not encourage him to play pro football. "Pro ball wasn't well thought of then," Mel recalled. "My coaches felt I would be getting in with the wrong kind of crowd— drinking, gambling, that kind of thing. They tried to talk me out of turning pro."

But the money talked louder than the coaches. Hein signed the Providence contract and dropped it in a mail box on the Washington State campus in Pullman, Washington. Then he accompanied the State basketball team, on which he played center, to Spokane, where they were scheduled to play Gonzaga. The Gonzaga basketball coach was Red Flaherty, who during the football season played end for the New York Giants. At halftime, Flaherty slapped Hein on the back.

"Glad you signed with us," Flaherty said. "I think the contract the Giants sent you is a good one."

Hein stared at Flaherty. "I never got any contract from the Giants," he said. "I figured they didn't want me so I signed with Providence. I mailed the contract this afternoon."

"How much did they offer you?" Flaherty asked.

"One hundred and thirty-five dollars a game," Mel told him candidly.

Flaherty was stunned. "Why, I know the Giants will pay you one hundred and fifty dollars a game," he said. "Look, I'll get in touch with the Giants tomorrow. Meanwhile, see if you can get that Providence contract back from the post office somehow. If you can, tear it up and don't do anything till I get in touch with you."

How could he get a letter back from the Post Office? Mel called the Pullman postmaster and explained what had happened. Sorry, the postmaster told him, but the letter was already on its way east. But the postmaster said that he might be able to get the letter back by sending a telegram ahead to the Providence postmaster, asking him to return the envelope when it arrived. Amazingly, the strategy worked. The Providence postmaster, alerted by the wire, returned Hein's contract. Mel ripped it up and promptly signed with the Giants. The Providence franchise collapsed a year later.

The Giants soon discovered that while Hein was one of the first football players from the Northwest to try pro football, he was going to be a splendid pro. Mel, at only 198 pounds, was light for a linebacker, but he had great speed. A sprinter in high school, he quickly proved that he was not only the fastest lineman on the Giant squad but could run with the swiftest ends and backs. And Hein knew his fundamentals. He blocked well and tackled with frightening finality.

Despite his promise, Hein did not play in the Giants' first few games. He sat on the bench. But when veteran George Murtagh, the regular, was injured, Mel went in to replace him. Hein was badly fooled on a few plays, but managed to come out of the game alive. The next week, when the Giants took a 27-7 beating from the Green Bay Packers, Hein was back on the bench. But the week after that, against the Chicago Bears, he made the starting lineup for the first time. He held the job until he retired.

Hein played heroically against the Bears that day. All he had to contend with was the greatest fullback of that era, Bronko Nagurski, and the most celebrated open-field runner of all time, Red Grange. The Bears won, 6-0, but Chicago Coach George Halas recognized that he had witnessed the birth of a new NFL star.

"Usually," Halas said, "you look for the rookies on another team and then take advantage of them. We tried working on Hein. But from the beginning he was too smart. We'd think he'd overshifted and we'd try a play to the short side. Wham! Hein is pulling our man down. We'd try a short pass thinking he'd rush, and he'd either bat it down or intercept. Even as a rookie, there was no one like him."

Later in the season, the Giants played the Bears again. The result was the same. Chicago won, 12-6. But again Hein stood out in defeat. Once, the Bears had a first down on the New York 1-foot line. Hein was in on every tackle as the Giants held Nagurski on four consecutive plunges and took the ball away on their 8-yard line.

Following the Bear game, Hein and the Giants took on the other Western powerhouse, the Packers. Mel quickly made a believer out of the Green Bay coach, Curly Lambeau. "George Trafton of the Bears may be the best center in the league," Lambeau said, "but this Hein isn't far behind him. He does everything right. And he does everything instinctively. He has a genius for diagnosing plays. He's always where he can do the most harm. He plays sixty minutes and has more left at the end than a lot of guys have when they start."

Throughout his long pro career, Mel Hein seemed to be forever locked in championship combat with the Bears or the Packers. Many of those games were classics of pitiless power football. In 1933, for example, the Giants played the Bears for the first NFL championship. Early in the first quarter, New York's quarterback, Harry Newman, called a secret play named the "Hein Special." With a tricky offensive shift, the Giants went from their standard single-wing to the T-formation. They did so in such a way that Hein was at one end of the line and thus became an eligible pass receiver. Mel handed the ball to quar-

Mel played on both offense and defense when he was starring for the Giants. On offense, he was a center.

terback Newman in the T-formation snap. But Newman didn't keep the ball. He plopped it right back in Hein's big hands. Then, pretending he still had the ball, Newman faded back as if to pass. As he did so, Harry "accidentally" lost his footing and fell down. The Bears' 250-pound tackle, George Musso, promptly fell on top of him.

All the while, the plan was for Hein to walk down the field with the football hidden until his blockers could wipe out the Chicago safetyman

and give him a clear path to the goal line. But, in
his anxiety, Mel became overeager. He began to
run too soon, alerting Chicago safetyman Carl
Brumbaugh, who tackled him on the Bear 15
after a 30-yard gain. Given this reprieve, the Bears
held, taking the ball away. The score changed
hands six times in the game but the Bears went
on to win, 23-21.

In 1938, Hein redeemed himself for this mistake. He didn't do it against the Bears but against
the equally formidable Packers. Green Bay had
two marvelous passers in Cecil Isbell and Arnie
Herber, as well as a fantastic end in Don Hutson
and a hard runner in Clark Hinkle. But if the
Packers had the league's best offense, the Giants
had the staunchest defense.

As usual, the defense won. The decisive play
came when Hein intercepted an Isbell pass and
thundered 50 yards for a touchdown. It was the
first time he scored in his pro career.

Several weeks later, the Packers played the
Giants again. This time the stakes were high—
the championship of the NFL. At the beginning
of the game, Green Bay seemed to point its plays
right at the kingpin of the New York defense, Mel
Hein. And to everyone's amazement, the Packers
rolled steadily down the field. Coach Steve Owen
of the Giants was so alarmed that he called Hein
over for a sideline conference.

"You all right?" Owen asked Mel.

"Don't worry," Hein replied. "I'm letting them
get the short yardage. I'm making them commit

themselves before I commit myself. I'm not going to let Hutson get behind me for a touchdown pass."

Eventually, Mel's tactics paid off. The Packer attack was blunted. Before the half ended, the Giants led, 16-7. But Hein had been carried off the field with a concussion after receiving a kick in the head. Mel could not remember where he was; he didn't even know his name. Without Hein in the New York lineup, Green Bay came swarming back to the take the lead, 17-16. Then the Giants took command again, 23-17. At that point, Mel Hein trotted back on the field to face the Packers' last offensive drive. Immediately, the New York defense stiffened—and a few minutes later the Giants were champions. A few weeks later, Mel Hein was named the Most Valuable Player in the NFL for the 1938 season.

Over the years, Hein has become a symbol of durability much like the great New York Yankee baseball star, Lou Gehrig. Playing sixty minutes of football as he did, Mel inevitably sustained injuries. But his ability to play despite the aches and pains was remarkable. As a result the legend has sprouted that Hein never missed a game. It's an impressive story, but not quite true. In 1936, Mel sat out a game against the Chicago Cardinals.

Usually, if Hein left a game, he was on a stretcher. In a game at the Polo Grounds on December 7, 1941, players on both teams became aware of frequent announcements over the stadium's public address system, urging all servicemen to report to their bases. "We had an inkling something was up," Hein remembered, "but we didn't know what. Nobody had portable radios in those days."

Early in the second half, Hein suffered a brain concussion when an opponent's elbow landed in his face. Hein had to be rushed to the hospital.

"I was all doped up with medication," Mel said later, "and I didn't come out of it until the next day. One of our other players, Nello Falaschi, was in the next hospital bed. He had hurt his leg in the same game. He told me that Pearl Harbor had been bombed by the Japanese, and that we were at war. I was still groggy and didn't believe him until he showed me a newspaper with the headlines. I guess I'm one of the very few who was a day late hearing about the attack."

Two weeks later, when the Giants met the Bears for the NFL title, Mel was back in the lineup. But for the first time, he wore a face mask.

Hein finally decided to quit after the 1942 season. He took a job as head football coach at Union College, about 150 miles from New York City. He soon found that the war had depleted the manpower at Union. Only thirteen candidates turned out for football so the sport was dropped.

The Giants had retired Mel's Number 7 when he quit, but Coach Owen persuaded him to come back as a weekend player. It was difficult to stay in shape and keep on top of all the Giant plays, but Hein managed to do so for three years. Then, after the 1945 season, Mel Hein retired for good. He had played longer than any Giant, before or since, and helped his team win seven Eastern Division championships and two NFL titles. Only Sammy Baugh, the great Washington Redskin passer, had a longer NFL career than Hein. Sammy played sixteen years to Mel's fifteen.

Mel never really left football, though. He was a line coach with the Los Angeles Dons of the All-America Football Conference in 1947 and 1948. Then he held the same job with the New York Yankees of the AAFC in 1949 and the NFL's Los Angeles Rams in 1950. In 1951, he became line coach at the University of Southern California, where he remained for fifteen years. In 1966 he returned to professional football as the American Football League's supervisor of officials—a job he still holds.

Mel's children have also shown outstanding athletic ability. His daughter, Sharon Lynn, was a champion backstroke swimmer at the University of Southern California. His son, Mel, Jr., at one time held the American indoor pole-vaulting record of 16 feet, $5\frac{1}{2}$ inches.

Unlike some old-time football players, who grumble about being born a generation too soon for the big bonuses, Mel Hein isn't bitter, even though he confesses that it wasn't until after his twelfth season in the NFL that he earned as much as $5,000 a season. Nor does Hein believe that the players of his day were better than the modern pros.

Mel with Mel, Jr. who rose to heights in a different sport—as a record-breaking pole vaulter.

"Players going into pro ball now are much better equipped physically than in my day," he said, "specifically because of better high school football programs and body-building techniques. Today's players are bigger and faster and have a greater knowledge of football techniques when they reach the pro level. Pro football today is better than it was when I played it. I don't mean to take anything away from the players of the 1930s and 1940s. If we had the same advantages as today's players, I think we'd be just as outstanding. I honestly don't see any reason why I couldn't play linebacker in the pros. I think I could adjust to the way the game is played."

BULLDOG TURNER

The 1939 college All-America football team had the usual quota of great players. Among them were quarterback Paul Christman of Missouri, halfbacks Nile Kinnick of Iowa and Tommy Harmon of Michigan. The center on that All-America eleven was John Schiechl of Santa Clara. Schiechl subsequently went on to a modest career in professional football, drifting from the Pittsburgh Steelers to the Detroit Lions to the Chicago Bears and, finally, to his last port of call, the San Francisco Forty-Niners.

The name of another center, Clyde "Bulldog" Turner, did not appear on the 1939 All-America lists—mainly because he labored in relative obscurity at a virtually unknown college, Hardin-Simmons, in Abilene, Texas. Yet, while few fans still remember John Schiechl, Bulldog Turner still stands unchallenged as one of the National Football League's all-time great linebacking stars.

In 1939, Turner was the first draft choice of the Chicago Bears. The sportswriters could not believe it when the Bears' owner-coach, George Halas, ignored a flock of better-publicized college players to pick a "nobody" like the center-linebacker from "that little Texas school with the two names." But Halas knew what he was doing. He realized that this big, strong Texan would be the new Gibraltar of the Bear line, on both offense and defense.

Halas, of course, was right. Just as the New York Giants' Mel Hein was the leading center-linebacker of the 1930s, Bulldog Turner dominated the NFL at the same position during the 1940s. Turner played thirteen seasons with the Bears, from 1940 through 1952. During that span, he made first-string All-League team six times—in 1941, 1942, 1943, 1944, 1946 and 1948—and helped Chicago win four NFL championships. During the 1942 season, Turner made pro football history when he intercepted eight passes and became the only linebacker ever to lead the NFL in interceptions. After his retirement from active competition, he was named to the Pro Football Hall of Fame.

Bulldog Turner joined the Bears three weeks after the team had begun training during the summer of 1940. Prior to that, he had been with the College All-Stars.

"I was," Bulldog admitted, "the most ignorant guy who ever reported to any pro camp. I didn't know much about the refinements of the game. I just felt nobody could beat me at anything. I had never paid much mind to those All-America teams. I knew I was the best college football player in the Southwest, and I figured the Bears were lucky to get me."

Turner caused a sensation in his first practice

session with the Bears. Traditionally, Coach Halas would line up his veteran starters. He would start by bellowing, "Give me a center!" Traditionally, the *regular* center would bounce out of the player ranks and take his place over the ball. That season Chicago's regular center was Frank Bausch, a tough pro. But when Halas shouted, "Give me a center!" Bausch never had a chance. He was beaten to the ball by Bulldog Turner, who had no idea that rank had its privileges, and that he had violated protocol. "Coach wanted a center," Turner said later, "and I figured I was a center, so . . ."

Bausch never did get his job back. Turner became the Bears' starting center on offense and a linebacker on defense. Even now, some Chicago front office people who rate Turner tops at center are not quite sure about Bulldog's credentials as a linebacker. But Turner has no doubts. "I have the bruises to prove it," he says. Defensively, the Bears used the 6-2-2-1 and 5-3-2-1 defensive line-ups. In both formations, Bulldog played outside right linebacker. "On runs," he said, "my responsibility was to make tackles. On passes, I had to cover a lot of fast halfbacks man to man. That's one of the differences between the way we played linebacker then and the way they play it today in the pros. In my time, corner linebackers had a much harder job on pass coverage. We were almost comparable to today's corner halfbacks."

Turner did not look like any cornerback the world has ever seen. He was a bulky, muscular man—232 pounds in his prime. But he was astonishingly quick for his size. Until he began to slow down a bit after about eight seasons in the NFL, he was considered the fastest lineman in the league. Coach Halas made sure Turner maintained his speed. He would fine Bulldog $50 for every week he weighed more than 232 pounds. And since Turner began his pro career at an annual salary of only $2,250, he watched his weight scrupulously.

Turner prefers to be remembered as a linebacker more than as a center. "Look," he said, "that's the only recognition a guy like me could get—making tackles while backing up the line. I was just as good on offense as I was on defense, I think, but offensive centers just get lost in the crowd."

Until his last two seasons in the NFL, Turner played both ways. In 1951 and 1952, however, he played offense only—with one exception. In 1951 the Bears played the old Chicago Cardinals (now the St. Louis Cardinals) in what was then a bitter crosstown rivalry. The Cardinals were touting a center and a linebacker for All-NFL honors, and there had been some talk that both of these players were better than Bulldog Turner had ever been. Turner was allowed to play offense *and* defense that day. He put in sixty tremendous minutes and demonstrated what a genuine All-Leaguer was like. The Bears won, 24-14.

Like all the Bears, Turner was a terrifying tackler. He was confident, almost cocksure of his ability. But the ability was there. When he hit a ball carrier, he practically tore the man apart limb from limb. Yet there was a gentle side to Bulldog Turner, too. It did not surface often—it couldn't in the ferociously competitive world of pro football—but Turner had the bigness of character to value an opponent who had earned his respect.

One such opponent was Ken Strong of the New York Giants. In the 1930s, Strong had been one of the league's outstanding running backs. Then he retired. But during World War II, when there was a shortage of players, Strong came out of retirement at the age of thirty-seven to help the Giants as a kicking specialist. In 1943 the Giants played the Bears in an exhibition game. Strong kicked off and wheezed downfield, trying to help make the tackle. Suddenly Bulldog Turner loomed in front of him. Turner could have destroyed Strong with one crunching block. Instead he wheeled and picked another, less vulnerable target. "I can't hit you," he told Strong. "You're just too darned old."

After the 1951 season, Turner quit as a player. The Bears staged a big "Bulldog Turner Day" at Wrigley Field, then gave him a job as an assistant coach. But during the 1952 exhibition season, the Bears ran short of offensive tackles. Coach Halas

Bulldog played with some of the best teams in NFL history. Here he lines up at center with quarterback Sid Luckman and the rest of the Bears' 1943 championship backfield.

promptly reactivated Turner and started him at offensive right tackle, where he played every minute of 1952. "Boy, that was a snap, playing tackle," Turner said. "At least . . . compared to being a linebacker."

When he reviews his illustrious NFL career, Bulldog's scores of memorable tackles and blocks run together. What he really remembers are the moments of glory that a big linebacker seldom experiences. "Once," he recalled, "in the late 1940s, I intercepted one of Sammy Baugh's passes on our four-yard-line and ran ninety-six yards for a touchdown. It wasn't one of those straight runs down the sideline, either. I had to cut back across the field three times and use my blockers. Let me tell you, I was in a broken field—me! Baugh finally jumped on my back on the Redskin seven-yard line. But I just dragged him over the goal line. He wasn't going to stop me that close."

Baugh and Turner share a common heritage. Both are Texans and both played high school football in the same town, known by the picturesque name of Sweetwater. Turner was born on March 10, 1919, in Plains, Texas, which he has described as "one of the last frontier towns." Later his family moved to Sweetwater. At Sweetwater High School, Turner played only one year of football— as a 155-pound blocking back. With so little football experience, he was ignored by recruiters from the major colleges in the Southwest. There were no scholarship offers. "Nobody wanted me," Turner said.

But Turner and a friend, A. J. Roy, were determined to play college football. Roy had been asked to try out for the Hardin-Simmons team, and he got an invitation for Turner, too. The try-out was to be held early in the fall. All that summer the two young players trained grimly for their chance. To cheer themselves up in the oppressive Texas heat, they gave each other nicknames. A. J. Roy was "Tiger" and Clyde Turner became "Bulldog." They would shout to each other, "That the hardest you can hit, Bulldog?" Or, "Try that one again, Tiger!"

Both Roy and Turner made the Hardin-Simmons team, and Turner's nickname stuck with him. Later some people tried to glamorize the story by saying he had gotten the name because he loved to "bulldog" steers. "The nickname did me a lot of good," Turner admitted. "Got me a lot of publicity. You know, most football people still don't even know my real first name."

At Hardin-Simmons, Bulldog became a center and linebacker. He played in the first college game he ever saw. By his senior year, he weighed a solid 215 pounds.

With the Bears, Bulldog played for a team with a tradition of tough, imaginative linebacking. It was while he was with Chicago that the Bears invented that most colorful of all linebacking maneuvers, the "red dog." In recent years, "red-dogging" has become a widely used defensive tactic. The principle is brutally simple. Normally, four defensive linemen rush the passer. To confound the offensive blockers and to put greater pressure on the quarterback, one or more linebackers join the front four in a devilishly orchestrated rush. The "red-doggers" try to burst through the spaces between the blockers. The maneuver is also called "shooting the gaps," "blitzing" and "storming." But the name that has really captured the popular fancy is "red-dogging."

Actually, the "red-dog" began quite accidentally, according to Turner. In 1949 Bear fullback Ed "Catfoot" Cody found himself playing linebacker for the first time. On one play, Cody decided to improvise. Recklessly, he charged across the line of scrimmage into the offensive backfield of the Chicago Cardinals. The Cardinal blockers, who had never seen the tactic used before, did not attempt to stop him. Cody was allowed to descend unopposed on the quarterback, Paul Christman.

Again and again Cody came slashing through the bewildered Cardinals. By the time the game was over he had dumped Christman for thirteen losses all by himself, prompting the Bears' defensive coach, Hunk Anderson, to say, "Cody looked like a mad dog coming through there."

Recognizing that Cody had stumbled onto a defensive stratagem with limitless possibilities, Anderson developed a system that would allow him to unleash his "mad dogs" in a disciplined way. Quickly, a code emerged. When one linebacker rushed, it was a "white dog." When two linebackers rushed, Anderson called it a "blue dog." When all three rushed, that was a "red dog." Since then the term "red dog" has come to mean rushing by *any* linebacker.

Bulldog Turner stayed in professional football after he finally retired in 1952. In 1953 he became an assistant coach at Baylor University, then returned to the Bears for five years as an assistant coach in charge of the offensive line. In 1959 he was out of football for the first time since his high school days. He went back to his ranch in Gatesville, Texas. Then, in 1962, he returned to pro ball as head coach of the American Football League's New York Titans, the forerunners of the Jets. It was a year of aggravation. The Titans did not have a quarterback. Often their owner, the late Harry Wismer, did not pay his bills. After one season, Turner resigned and went back to Texas.

Even so, Bulldog has no regrets. He's content on his 1,200-acre spread, where he raises quarterhorses and thoroughbreds and his wife breeds tiny Chihuahua dogs. Turner still maintains an interest in pro football and its stars. "I'm fifty-one years old now," he said recently, "and I guess that's the age where you don't want to be forgotten. I don't want to brag, but I honestly don't think I ever saw a man I couldn't beat on the football field—offense or defense. Maybe there were better players than I was. But I think I did pretty well for a country boy."

RAY NITSCHKE

December 31, 1962. The Green Bay Packers beat the New York Giants, 16-7, for the NFL championship on a wickedly cold day in Yankee Stadium. The key plays of the game were made not by Packer quarterback Bart Starr, not by Green Bay's "Golden Boy" halfback, Paul Hornung, but by the team's omnipresent middle linebacker, 240-pound Ray Nitschke. In the first quarter, with the Giants in possession on the Green Bay 15-yard line, seemingly en route to a touchdown, Nitschke rushed New York quarterback Y. A. Tittle savagely on one of the Packers' few blitzes. Nitschke put one hand up and deflected Tittle's pass into the hands of Green Bay's left linebacker Dan Currie. In the second quarter, Nitschke recovered a fumble on the Giant 28, and three plays later Green Bay was in for a touchdown. In the third quarter, Nitschke recovered another fumble on the Giant 42, setting up the Packers' final points, a field goal by Jerry Kramer. After the game, Nitschke was named the game's Most Valuable Player.

Later that evening, at a victory party in Greenwich Village, Ray Nitschke sat on the floor, talking quietly about the game and the brutal

Nitschke is riding high in a sports car he received from Sport *magazine for being MVP in the championship game.*

weather conditions that had prevailed. Up close, Nitschke is a large, soft-spoken man, balding, wearing horn-rimmed glasses. He held up his hands. They were still so swollen from the cold that the flesh virtually covered Nitschke's ring. To remove the ring, he would have had to have cut it off. Some guests at the party could not believe that this was really Ray Nitschke, the so-called "wildman" of the Green Bay Packers.

December 31, 1967. The Green Bay Packers defeated the Dallas Cowboys, 21-17, for the NFL championship. In the winners' dressing room, television commentator Tom Brookshier, a former defensive back with the Philadelphia Eagles, brought one of the Packer heroes, Ray Nitschke, to the microphone for an interview. Nitschke was half-dressed and disheveled, perspiration still running down his face.

"And here's Green Bay's *madman*, Ray Nitschke," began Brookshier, with a jolly smile.

Ray Nitschke did not return the smile. He bristled. "I'm not a madman," he told Brookshier brusquely. "I just enjoy football."

Hastily, Brookshier changed tack and began to discuss the details of the game itself with the great middle linebacker of the Packers, as if "madman" hadn't been mentioned at all. Nitschke submitted to the questioning patiently—once he had let the whole country know that he was disturbed when referred to as some kind of psychopath in cleats and shoulder pads.

In reality, there are two Ray Nitschkes. One is the perfect gentlemen at the party. The other is the hard-driving, ham-handed linebacker whom the Cowboys accused of playing "dirty football" when he seemed to kick Dallas running back Don Perkins after Perkins went down in the final quarter of the hard-fought 1967 championship game.

Nitschke recognizes that he helped create his image as a boisterous hatchetman. Long ago, Ray did some things he would just as soon forget. "I was real obnoxious, real rowdy years ago," Ray once admitted. "I was mad all the time and I took it out on everybody. I was a hard guy to get along with. My father died when I was three and my mother died when I was thirteen. I was brought up by my brother. He was good to me, but I never had any real discipline. I grew up belting the other kids in the neighborhood. Nobody told me what to do or what not to do. I felt I was somebody who didn't have anything, so I took it out on other people." Nitschke conceded that he behaved this way throughout high school and college—and even after he joined the Packers. Thus the "wildman" characterization began.

But Nitschke changed. Those close to the Packers credit the influence of his wife, Jackie, whom he married in 1963. Ray himself said simply, "I matured. It just took me a little longer to grow up. Now I don't go around hating people—and now I don't want to be known as an animal or a dirty player, because I'm not. I never actually tried to kick Perkins that day in Dallas. It may have looked that way, but the only reason I swung my leg the way I did was because I was disgusted with myself that I didn't bring him down. Yes, I hit hard. You've got to. Football is like war. It's a kind of survival course. If you're not anxious to hit people, you don't belong on the field. When they run a play at you the second time, you want them to have more respect for you than when they ran the first. You've got to make it so they never forget you're there. You can't play the game unless you enjoy contact. But nobody wants to be

Nitschke puts fear into opponents.

known as a guy who would deliberately hurt another player."

In the last few years, Nitschke has achieved
pre-eminence among the National Football
League's middle linebackers. Among players in
the 1960s, he is considered the best practitioner of
the game's most difficult defensive position. To be
sure, Tommy Nobis of the Atlanta Falcons and
Dick Butkus of the Chicago Bears are strong chal-
lengers. And since both are younger men they
may displace Nitschke sooner rather than later.
But according to the men who know middle linebackers best, Nitschke was still number one in the
1960s.

Nitschke was, in fact, voted the finest middle
linebacker in football—over Butkus and Nobis—
in a magazine poll taken in 1967. The judges, five
former great pro linebackers, felt that Ray best
supplied the strength, quickness, speed, toughness, intelligence and leadership that a great middle linebacker must possess. One of the voters, Joe
Schmidt, once a mighty linebacker for the Detroit
Lions, cast his vote for Nitschke and explained,
"I'd say that Ray is the finest in the game. He is
particularly quick, although probably not as fast
as Nobis. He has amazing lateral quickness and
mobility, and that is of prime importance to the
middle linebacker."

Former Baltimore Colt Bill Pellington and
ex-Los Angeles Ram Les Richter made it three out
of five votes for Nitschke.

"A guy like Nitschke has been sensational,"

said Pellington, "coming up with the big interception or big tackle or big fumble recovery. He's been very instrumental in the Packers' developing such a fine defense. Coming up with the big plays is a kind of leadership, but Nitschke takes it one step further. He's the core of that team; he's able to direct it, he's such an inspiring sort of a guy. He always puts out."

Richter added, "It's not so much physical speed, or even quickness, in Nitschke's case. It seems to me that he just has the desire to make the play, an ability to get to the right point in the shortest period of time. I don't care if he walks or runs or flies, just as long as he is the first man to get to the play. And Nitschke usually is."

When the All-NFL teams were picked, Nitschke's name usually led all the rest. He was named to the Associated Press and United Press International All-Pro teams in 1964, UPI All-Pro in 1965, and AP and UPI again in 1966. The NFL players named Nitschke the league's outstanding linebacker for 1967.

Ironically, Ray Nitschke, scourge of pro quarterbacks, began his football career as a quarterback. At Proviso High School in Maywood, Illinois, a Chicago suburb, Ray played for former Notre Dame star Andy Puplis. Nitschke did not play quarterback with much finesse. He did not execute hand-offs with dexterity, nor was he a pinpoint passer, but he loved to hit. Ray weighed 190 pounds then, and he kept trying to run over everybody. As one Chicago journalist wrote, "He didn't run to daylight, he ran to flesh." Despite his inelegance as a quarterback, Nitschke was effective. He guided Proviso High to a suburban league title, made the All-State team, then went off to try his luck at the University of Illinois in 1954.

"At Illinois I was switched to fullback as a sophomore, and I played linebacker on defense," Nitschke recalled. Ray did have one moment of offensive glory, though. In his sophomore year, he scored four touchdowns on long runs against Iowa State. None of the runs involved clever footwork. Nitschke simply burst into the clear and, shedding tacklers along the way, powered toward the end zone. But for the most part, his greatest value to the Illini came from backing up the line.

Nitschke was not an All-America at Illinois. In fact, he did not have a reputation outside the Big Ten. Thus the Packers waited until the third round to draft him for the 1958 season. Unlike Dick Butkus, who followed Nitschke to Illinois and the pros, Ray had a long, unhappy rookie season. He played as a regular, all right, but not because Scooter McLean, then the head coach at Green Bay, had any great faith in him. "Our regular middle linebacker, Tom Bettis, was hurt," Nitschke recalled, "so I started the first eight games for the Packers. In that eighth game, the Redskins beat us pretty badly—that was the day Johnny Olszewski of the Washington Redskins gained 156 yards against us. They blamed it on me, and I didn't start any more that season. I didn't hold it against anybody, though. That's a rookie for you—he's going to get the blame."

Two years later, however, Vince Lombardi was running the Packers and Nitschke replaced Tom Bettis by mid-season. Excluding the last three games of 1963, when he was out with a broken right arm, Nitschke has been the Green Bay middle linebacker ever since.

When Lombardi first took Nitschke in hand, he felt that Ray had all the natural ability to become a fine linebacker, but that he needed to develop more self-discipline, to learn how to read keys, to understand how to dissect a rival offense.

Nitschke learned. "Most of the time I key on the fullback," he explained. "The fullback and the center. But it changes with the personnel I play against. A triple wing or slot formation, for example, would change my responsibility." Against a team like the Dallas Cowboys, calling defensive signals presents a special challenge to Nitschke. "The formation determines the defense I call, and I may change my original call if I see a change in the other team's offensive alignment. Calling signals against the Cowboys is quite a job, because they show such a wide variety of formations."

But no matter what signals he calls, Nitschke expects to give and take hard knocks. "A middle linebacker is hit on *every* play," he once said, not without pride. "He should be in on a majority of tackles if he's doing his job. The interior linemen are keeping the blockers off him—or they should' be—so the middle linebacker ought to be free to

hit that ball carrier most of the time."

Nitschke goes full-tilt, even in practice, and at times he has been as hard on his teammates as he is on the opposition. In 1962, four days before the Packers were to face the New York Giants for the NFL championship, Coach Vince Lombardi was dissatisfied with the way practice was going. Lombardi shouted at his defensive unit, "Hit those guys like they're Giants!" The very next play, Nitschke took Lombardi at his word. He crashed head-on into Jim Ringo, just after the Packers' All-League center had snapped the ball to quarterback Bart Starr. "I popped him," Ray admitted, "and I popped him good."

In "popping" Ringo, Nitschke nearly removed his teammate's head from his shoulders. Ringo sustained a severely pinched muscle in his neck and almost was unable to play against the Giants. Yet Nitschke did not mean to injure Ringo. "I couldn't see Jim there at all," Ray said. "To me he was Ray Wietecha, the Giants' center. That's why I busted him good."

Nitschke can take as well as give. In college, he refused to wear a face mask, deriding it as a device for sissies. Against Ohio State, he was wiped out with a blind-side block on a kickoff return. The blocker knocked out several of Nitschke's teeth. Ray never left the game, though. He stuffed wads of cotton into the bloody holes in his gums and

Off the field, Ray, shown with his sons, is a pleasant guy to be around.

played a full game of furious football. After the game, Ray spent half an hour searching the playing field for his lost teeth. Why? "They belong to me," he said grimly.

Nitschke's strength and durability remain a source of amazement to the Packers. Once, while the Packers were practicing, a 25-foot-high steel tower used by coaches and photographers to get a bird's-eye view of the field was blown over by a strong wind. Nitschke was standing near the tower as it toppled, and the huge structure fell right on him. Fortunately, Ray had just put on a helmet a moment before. When the tower fell, a steel spike bashed in his helmet. The spike grazed his left temple. According to legend, Coach Lombardi strode over to the fallen tower and asked who was pinned under it.

"Nitschke," came the reply.

Lombardi grinned toothily. "Aagh! Let's get back to football," he said. "Nitschke will be all right."

Ray still sees nothing wrong with Lombardi's bullish attitude. "I was okay, and coach knew it." But just to make sure, Lombardi had the tower cemented into place the very next day.

Like many of the Packers, Nitschke did not play his best in 1968. Even so, Packer fans voted him the team's Most Valuable Player for the sec-

Ray's vicious tackles are just part of his fearless approach to football, as Oakland's Hewritt Dixon learns in the 1968 Super Bowl game.

ond straight year. At the award ceremony, the fans learned for the first time that Nitschke had played despite severe pain throughout the season. A chronic neck injury kept acting up, and Ray simply was not himself. "He was playing under wraps," explained new Packer Coach Phil Bengtson, who replaced Lombardi. "By that I mean he was not in the best of shape. Seeing him in the trainer's room every morning, and knowing what he had to bear up under, I thought it was an excellent display of the type of attitude we must have on the Packers."

Looking to the future, Nitschke said, "I'm just as good a football player as I've ever been. I've had minor injuries, which are part of the game. Naturally, I would have liked to have made some bigger plays in 1969 than I did. And, of course, you always want to get better and improve. I still have the zest and zeal to play the game—so I haven't given up on myself or the Green Bay Packers."

Forewarned is forearmed. But then Ray Nitschke's opponents are always on guard.

MAXIE BAUGHAN

Maxie Baughan grew up in Bessemer, Alabama, a steel-mill city often referred to as "the Pittsburgh of the South." Bessemer is the perfect place for Baughan to call home. For, at 230 pounds, the squat and balding right-corner linebacker of the Los Angeles Rams is truly a "man of steel." He looks as though he had been forged right there in one of Bessemer's mills.

Strangely enough, the All-Pro star got his start in high school football as a quarterback on offense —as well as a linebacker on defense. Maxie weighed 162 pounds then. "I was a little bitty thing who threw the ball about fifteen yards," Baughan recalled about the days when he quarterbacked Bessemer's T-formation team.

But on defense, he was something else. "The college scouts liked my linebacking," Maxie said, "and since I had big feet they figured my body would grow accordingly. So I got a scholarship to Georgia Tech."

Tech Coach Bobby Dodd soon found that he had recruited a great one. As a senior in 1959, Baughan set a Georgia Tech record by making 124 tackles in a single season. He was voted Southeastern Conference Lineman of the Year and named to the All-America team. Coach Dodd called Baughan "one of the most consistently great players I've coached in twenty-seven years."

In 1960, Maxie signed with the Philadelphia Eagles, who had made him their second-round choice in the college draft. Before long, Baughan had developed into one of the toughest young outside linebackers in the NFL.

"Max is a real solid pro," said his coach, Joe Kuharich of the Eagles. "He's not as gifted with speed, agility and size as most linebackers, but he has the overall know-how and—more important —he has that intangible we call football instinct. He seems to know where the point of impact will be. He's a tremendous competitor and leader."

For five of his six seasons with the Eagles, Baughan was a Pro Bowl choice and a consistent contender for All-NFL mention. Then, inexplicably, before the 1966 season he and defensive back Irv Cross were traded to the Rams for linebacker Fred Brown, defensive tackle Frank Molden and a draft choice.

With the Eagles, Maxie had stood out as a red-dogging linebacker who got to a quarterback as quickly as anyone. But with the Rams, he had to play a more disciplined game. The Los Angeles front four—led by Deacon Jones and Merlin Olsen—applied so much pressure on a quarterback that there was no need for linebackers to shoot the gaps. Maxie concentrated on dropping back with the receivers. He has said that learning to be in the right position on pass plays is the most important and difficult thing for a linebacker to master.

"You have to get position on the man moving out for the pass or you're dead," Maxie explained. "Otherwise it becomes a footrace between you and the receiver, and those halfbacks and ends can outrun a linebacker every time. You have to get position and stay with your man until you get help."

Baughan looked as if he needed help in more ways than one. "He looks like a fighter being patched up between rounds," said Ram Coach George Allen. "After each series of downs, some wound or injury seems to act up again. But Maxie always goes right back in with the defense."

Baughan always was an astonishingly durable football player. During his ten years in the NFL, he missed only two games. It wasn't as if Maxie didn't have any painful injuries; he had more than his share of them. But he played anyway. The two games he did miss were both played in 1964, while he was with the Philadelphia Eagles. He pulled a leg muscle in practice. "It felt as if I'd been shot," Baughan recalled. "It was the first time I found out I had muscles."

Maxie had already found out that he had bones. During the 1963 season he played most of the games with a fractured hand. "It made things pretty tough," he said. "I played with a cast on. There was no use sitting out any games because it didn't hurt except when I gripped. And you only have to grip on one out of every four

*An old quarterback, Maxie enjoys carry-
ing the ball after an interception.*

or five tackles. In pro football, I've always felt
that you must play with injuries unless they hurt
so much that it's impossible. There's a certain
amount of pain in every tackle, and you must get
accustomed to that fact right away, or you don't
make it in this league."

Baughan learned about injuries early in his pro
career. As a rookie in 1960, he had acquired a bad
shoulder in a game against the Forty-Niners. He
also had to limp around on an injured ankle. But
that didn't stop Baughan. Working with two veterans of the Eagle defense, halfback Tom Brookshier and tackle Marion Campbell, he matured
rapidly despite the physical handicaps. When the

Eagles beat the Detroit Lions, rookie Maxie played so well he was awarded the game ball. "For the first time," Maxie said, "I felt as if I was part of the team."

In 1961, Maxie continued to play with the chronic shoulder injury as well as a damaged wrist that required repeated cortisone injections by the Eagles' team physician. His teammates quickly recognized his toughness and began to make jokes about it. "Gee, look at Max," end Pete Retzlaff would say, "no black eyes this week, no cuts, no teeth missing, no ear chewed off."

Baughan would just smile as he answered, "Yeah, I'm getting so handsome I can't look in the mirror."

But there were frustrations during those early years, too—particularly at the hands of the New York Giants and their great quarterback, Y. A. Tittle. During a 1961 game between the Eagles and the Giants, Tittle and defensive back Erich Barnes combined on a special trick play. Barnes fled downfield as an extra receiver late in the first half, forcing Baughan to cover him man-for-man. Maxie couldn't quite match Barnes' great speed and Erich caught a 62-yard touchdown pass from Tittle that was the decisive play in a 38-21 Giant victory.

"It wasn't all Maxie's fault," said Philadelphia's defensive coach, Jerry Williams, now the head coach of the team. "He has good speed for a linebacker, but Barnes got a step on him and simply outran him for the ball."

Baughan had another "injury year" in 1967. During his second season with the Rams, he experienced cartilage problems with his right knee and bone chips rattled around in his right ankle. Although a corner linebacker's stock in trade is mobility, the hobbled Baughan remained the Rams' top defender with fifty-five unassisted tackles and twenty-six assists. Baughan also retained enough quickness to intercept four passes.

During that same 1967 season, Baughan became involved in a rare controversy over "signal-jamming." It occurred in Kezar Stadium, San Francisco, where the Rams were defeating their arch rivals, the Forty-Niners. The protagonists were Baughan, who was calling defensive signals for the Rams, and the Forty-Niners' quarterback, John Brodie.

As Brodie began calling a play at the line of scrimmage, he would shout out a color—for instance, blue. Then he would follow with the number of the play. After that the quarterback would bark, "Go, go, go!"

It had been pre-determined in the huddle that the Forty-Niners would start the play on the third "Go!" They never got a chance to do so, however. Across the line of scrimmage, Maxie Baughan was calling his own signals.

"Show!" he yelled. "Show!"

In a stadium of shouting fans, "show" can sound

With the Rams, Maxie was a leader on one of pro football's finest defensive teams.

very much like "go." It certainly did to the Forty-Niner offensive line, which lunged off-side. The Forty-Niner players and coaches immediately protested that Baughan had drawn them off-side by illegally "jamming" their signals. The officials agreed. They penalized the Rams for signal-jamming, but they also penalized the Forty-Niners for being off-side, nullifying the whole play.

After the game, Ram Coach George Allen changed the defensive signal from "Show" to "Sid" rather than risk further entanglement with Mark Duncan, the NFL's supervisor of officials. "There are two things you can't do as a defensive signal-caller," Duncan explained. "You can't use words that sound like offensive signals. And you can't adopt a quarterback's manner, his tone of voice, the sharp edge to his words."

But what bothered Maxie Baughan most of all was that he had incorrectly diagnosed John Brodie's original call! He thought Brodie had called a pass to the weak side, but the quarterback hadn't. By misreading the quarterback's intentions, Maxie felt he had committed a serious mistake. Especially since he had earned a reputation as one of the shrewdest defensive tacticians in the NFL.

He had gotten into difficulty in Philadelphia when he disagreed with the Eagles' philosophy of defense. "I didn't like the way they went about playing defense," said Baughan, who quite candidly admits that he and Eagle Coach Kuharich did not hit it off as well as they might have. "You disagree with the boss and someone has to go," Maxie said. "It was me."

Red-headed Maxie studied defense like a rookie even after he established himself with the Rams. In training camp, and during the season, he was never without a thick orange notebook with hundreds of pages of diagrams and reports. "I'll digest maybe two hundred pages on the next team we play," Baughan said. "And this is revolutionary. We didn't have anything like it in Philadelphia. Each team has ten or so basic offensive formations, but here I can show you fifteen to twenty variations off each one of these. You have to be familiar with all of them."

At home after practice, Baughan was a film critic. Every week he screened and analyzed two or three reels of film on the Rams' upcoming opponent. By week's end, he and his defensive comrades had their own "game plan"—just as the offensive unit did. Like all top linebackers, Baughan firmly believed that he had to react instinctively or all was lost. "We've got one-hundred and fifty different audibles I can call when I want to," he said, "and you just don't have time to think about them. If you do, you'll be left just standing there."

Maxie finished 1967 with two triumphs. He made consensus All-NFL despite his leg problems, and he played an outstanding game in the Pro Bowl. No blitzing is allowed in the All-Star game between the best players of the East and the West, because the offensive linemen cannot work together long enough. But straight-ahead pursuit is perfectly legal. And pursuit is what Maxie Baughan did superbly, bad leg or not.

On one play, with his West team trailing by three points, Baughan found himself chasing the East quarterback, Fran Tarkenton of the New York Giants, on one of Tarkenton's famous scrambles. Finally, Maxie made the forcing play. With Baughan closing in relentlessly, and with all escape hatches closed, Tarkenton had to get rid of the football. He threw his pass sooner than he wanted to, and he did not get much power behind the ball.

West defensive halfback Richie Petitbon of the Chicago Bears promptly intercepted the pass and ran seventy yards for the touchdown that put the West in front to stay. The last defender with a chance to stop Petitbon was Tarkenton himself. But Baughan was still there. Maxie blotted Fran out of the play with a key block—his second fine move in a few seconds—as Petitbon raced by to the goal line.

Soon after that, Baughan underwent surgery to repair his torn knee cartilage and to remove the loose bone chips from his ankle. A month after the operation, he was struggling to jog four or five miles a day, driving himself so that he would be ready for the 1968 season.

Maxie was ready. In 1968 he was an integral part of a Ram defense that allowed the fewest yards gained—3,118—of any team since the NFL went into the fourteen-game schedule. Baughan led all Ram linebackers with sixty-three tackles and assisted on thirty-four others. He made the Associated Press All-NFL team.

Thus, Baughan's ninth year was one of his best yet. In fact, the Rams felt that the Alabama strongman was still so good that they rewarded him with a new three-year contract. Maxie's tenth pro season looked like one of his best as the Rams won their first eleven games and appeared on their way to the Super Bowl. But disaster overtook the Rams. The team lost its final three regular season games, then was beaten by the Minnesota Vikings for the NFL's Western Conference title. In the Rams' last game before meeting the Vikings, Baughan severely strained the ligaments in his right knee. He made a brave effort to play against Minnesota, a team that likes to use its backs as pass receivers. Unable to cut or run with his usual agility, and thus unable to cover the Viking backs, Maxie had to leave the game. It was a bitter way to end a career. Shortly after the season finished, Maxie Baughan announced his retirement.

There had been many good days, however, and they are what Maxie—and his fans—will remember.

WAYNE WALKER

Season after season, for twelve years, Wayne Walker of the Detroit Lions has ranked among the quality outside linebackers in the National League. Whether Walker is *the* best in the NFL at his position, weak-side (right-side) linebacker, is open to debate. Wayne does not always make All-Pro first-string. But his consistent ability to play championship football is beyond question.

Wayne Walker, at age 34, is big, fast and tough. But all linebackers in pro football must be big, fast and tough or they do not remain in pro football very long. Not all of them, however, are as smart as Wayne Walker, who made the dean's list when he attended the University of Idaho and who now is considered the "thinking man's linebacker." When Walker talks about the indelicate art of backing up his side of the line, as he once did in painstaking detail to writer Berry Stainback, it is instructive to listen:

"The first thing a weak-side linebacker checks," Walker said, "is where the split end lines up, so you know what he can do to you. If he's set out four yards or so, you know he's getting ready for a good release into the secondary. You can't split out wide with him, even though if you did you could play him head-on and slow his release into your secondary. But if a linebacker follows the split end out wide, the quarterback calls an automatic and runs off tackle, where the linebacker should be.

"If you see the end is split two-and-a-half yards from the tackle," Walker went on, making X's and O's on a restaurant tablecloth, "the end can do two things. He can block back on you—we call that a 'crackback'—or he can get that good release. If he's only split out one yard from the weak-side tackle, that tells you he's gonna block down on your defensive end or release to the inside for a pass or to block on the other side. So you narrow down what the offense can do from where that split end lines up."

Gulp! It's as difficult as it sounds, which is why intelligent linebackers such as Wayne Walker keep their jobs year after year. They can "read" an offense in a few seconds and thus can react promptly and efficiently. But there's more to the way a linebacker plays his position, according to Walker.

"Okay, so you check the split end and narrow down the possibilities," he continued. "The rest of the offensive team is in a formation, and you know what plays they can run off it, so you narrow it down some more. You know the down and the yardage to go and their frequencies (what that team will usually do in a given situation), so you narrow it down again. Then you look around at their guards. You hear about guys tipping off

plays. Well, they do. A guard has to have his
weight up when he's charging, and his weight
back when he's pulling to lead interference or
pass blocking. So you narrow it down some more.
I 'key' by looking between the guard and tackle
at the near running back, the one on my side. He's
the guy who can hit you—and when he flares
out for a pass the linebacker has to cover him.

"On the snap you watch to see how that near
back comes at you. If he comes in a little circle,
he's gonna hook you—try to turn you in for a
slant or sweep around you. In that case you've got
to 'string it out'—you've got to force that blocker
out toward the sideline. You've got to control
that blocker, keep him in front of the ballcarrier.
The ballcarrier can't cut until the blocker has
moved the linebacker to one side. The longer the
linebacker can hold the play in there, the more
time he gives the secondary to come up.

"Sometimes," Walker went on, "the back will
just try to 'influence' you; he'll just set you up
for a pulling guard. That's the toughest thing to
read. At the last second that back veers around
you, so you lean out, and the guard's got you if
you can't recover. Then the best thing you can do
is throw yourself in front of the guard. That closes
the hole and forces the runner outside, where you
hope help will come. Even though you didn't
make the play, you had a part in it because you
sealed off your responsibility."

Granted, that is a lot of technical football for
a fan to digest. But it indicates the options that

Walker peers over the line before making a

swarm through the mind of an NFL linebacker
as he stands poised in that moment before a play
explodes.

Wayne Walker stands 6-feet 2-inches tall and
weighs anywhere from 224 to 228 pounds. Walker
can run; he has done 40 yards in 4.9 seconds,
which is as fast as some backs. But most of all,
Walker thinks.

During his career with the Lions, Walker has
earned respect all around the league as a crafts-
man—a good, solid, fundamental football player.

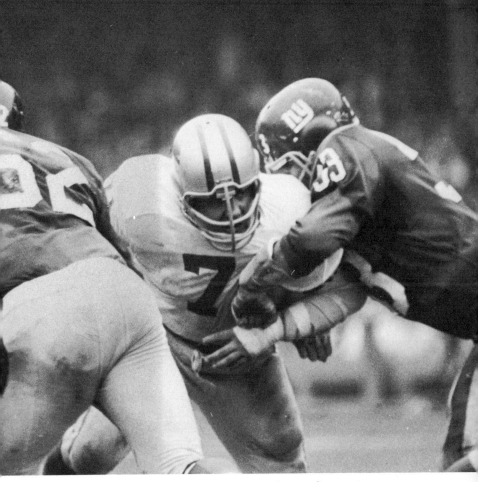

move. A linebacker's wrong move can be costly.

Some of his Detroit teammates say he does not get enough credit. "I think Wayne is the best outside linebacker in the game," said veteran cornerback Dick LeBeau, who plays on Walker's side. "He has more strength and more mobility than the others. Some have more strength and some have more mobility. But none of them has the combination of strength and mobility that Wayne has. I've talked to a lot of ends around the league and they all say the same thing."

As a weak-side linebacker, Walker gets to blitz

more than his strong-side counterpart. He can do so because the free safety stays behind him to cover a back who may fill the open spot left when Walker blitzes. Wayne's greatest blitzing day came in 1962, when the Lions demolished Green Bay in their annual Thanksgiving Day game. Walker said that the Lions blitzed on seven out of ten plays. "Our timing was perfect," he recalls. "We were hitting all the gaps right."

When he blitzes, Walker's assignment is to get to the quarterback and knock him down before he can get rid of the ball. But Wayne doesn't always head right for his target. He uses his first few blitzes to punish the blocker. Once he sees how the blocker intends to handle him, Walker storms in and tries to go right over him.

Wayne Walker of Boise, Idaho, joined the Lions in 1958, one of two University of Idaho football players chosen on the fourth round of the NFL's college draft. The other was guard Jerry Kramer of Sandpoint, picked by the Green Bay Packers. Walker and Kramer were the first Idaho players ever drafted by the pros. Neither Wayne nor Jerry had built major national reputations at Idaho, although both had received All-America mention and were selected for the annual East-West Shrine game and College All-Star game. Despite the lack of a long-standing

Wayne, No. 55, leads the blitz on the Rams' Frank Ryan. Teammates Bill Glass, No. 53, and Alex Karras, No. 77, help him.

pipeline to the pros, Walker believes that their coach at Idaho, Skip Stahley, prepared him and Jerry Kramer well for their NFL careers. "Stahley was a former coach in the pros," Walker said. "The only drawback to playing at a school like Idaho was that the pro scouts might never find you. I know the Lions never saw me play before they drafted me. I think Skip just sent them a film of one of our games, and they took his word that I could make it."

Walker played offensive center and middle linebacker at Idaho. The first indication that the Lions might have a prospective star came in the East-West game at Kezar Stadium in San Francisco. Walker made fifteen tackles, intercepted two passes and blocked a kick against top-flight college opposition.

Despite the fierce rivalry between the Lions and Packers, Walker and Kramer—who were roommates at Idaho—remained friends. Of course, Walker is careful to explain that he and Kramer did not often meet head on during a game. "I'm an outside linebacker," Wayne said, "and about the only time I run into a guard like Jerry is on a sweep play."

Naturally, there were exceptions. In 1960, Detroit's All-Pro middle linebacker, Joe Schmidt, was out with an injury. Walker was moved from the corner into Schmidt's position. As fate would have it, the Lions' opponent that Sunday was Green Bay. Kramer quickly said hello in his own physical fashion. "An offensive guard gets quite a few shots at the middle linebacker," Walker said, "and Jerry nailed me a few times." But late in the game, there was a turnabout. The Packers punted and Kramer came downfield to cover the kick. Walker noticed that his old roomie was "cruising"—that is, he had let up just a little bit. "I really hit him," Wayne recalled. "I must have knocked him ten feet in the air. They had to take him out of the game."

The quality of friendship is sometimes strained by pro football.

The presence of perennial All-Pro middle linebacker Joe Schmidt on the Detroit roster meant that Walker had to learn a new position in the pros. He had to adapt to playing on the corner. Wayne learned extremely rapidly. He did so by watching the great Schmidt's study habits and trying to emulate them. When Walker saw Joe studying game films on his own time, Wayne studied game films at home, too. When he saw Schmidt poring over playbooks while other Lions were out having a good time, Walker pored over playbooks, too. Wayne's intensity paid dividends. He became a starter in his third NFL game as a rookie in 1958.

In his first few years as a pro, Walker was a linebacker, period. At that time Detroit had a fine kicking specialist in Jim Martin. But when Martin began to grow old, Walker and quarterback Milt Plum shared the place-kicking assignment for the Lions. That was in 1962. Wayne was given the task of kicking the longer field goals, because he seemed to have the strong leg for them. But he was not exactly a raging success. He missed thirteen out of twenty-two field goal attempts. He had four kicks blocked. Ironically, Walker had no college experience as a kicker. At Idaho, Wayne snapped the ball from his position at offensive center as Jerry Kramer tried the field goals.

In 1963, Walker's place-kicking improved dramatically. Wayne attributed it to greater confidence. "If a guy's got confidence in the line in front of him," he said, "he ought to be able to kick seventy per cent of his field goals from inside the 50-yard line. If I don't have any blocked, my record ought to be that good. Sure, it's a mechanical thing. You get the timing and the teamwork with the guy holding the ball, and that's important." Walker's holder with the Lions in 1963 was quarterback Earl Morrall. "He's the best I've ever seen," Wayne said at the time. "He's got to hit an imaginary spot every time. If he's an inch off it can mean six yards over a distance of forty yards. That's more than enough to make a kick go wide."

Walker has never enjoyed the luxury of being just a kicker. Instead the versatile Lion star is more like Lou G oza once was. The Cleveland Brown star combined his kicking with playing offensive tackle when he was younger. "I'd probably do better kicking if I were just a specialist," Wayne said, speculatively, "but at least I get a chance to keep running on my kicking leg when I play linebacker. It's hard to come into a game cold and make a kick. It wouldn't be a bad idea, though,

to have some sort of bullpen for kicking specialists
—a place on the sidelines rigged up with a screen,
where kickers could try two or three boots to
warm up."

Walker has been involved in his share of controversy during his stay in the NFL. His worst
moment came in the spring of 1963, when he and
four Lion teammates were fined $2,000 each by
Commissioner Pete Rozelle for having made small
bets on the 1962 NFL championship game between the Packers and the Giants. Walker took his
punishment without flinching. "I'd have to go
along with the Commissioner," he said. "He was
justified in what he did. We were guilty of mis-
judgment."

And in 1966, Walker was involved in a furious
fist fight with Monty Stickles, the truculent tight
end who then played for the San Francisco Forty-
Niners. In the second quarter of the Detroit–San
Francisco game out in Kezar Stadium, Walker had
gone into the game expecting trouble from Stickles. "I watched movies of him against Dave Robinson of Green Bay, who I think is the best
outside linebacker in the league," Walker remembered. "On the first play of the game, Stickles hit
Robinson in the face with a forearm. Later Stickles did the same thing to Willie Davis of the
Packers. So I went into the game with the idea
that I wouldn't let him do that to me."

When Monty and Wayne met head-on, Stickles
threw a crushing block on Walker, knocked him
down, then jumped on him. Outraged, Wayne

protested to the umpire, who reportedly told him,
"Take care of it in your own way."

Walker did. He wheeled and punched Stickles
in the face. The umpire promptly threw Walker
out of the game, which made Wayne very mad.
He was even madder when Stickles, who was not
ejected, caught a touchdown pass to beat the Lions
with three seconds left in the game.

That same season, 1966, Wayne fell into another
deep kicking slump. By his own admission, he
never kicked worse. Walker hit only two of eight
field goal tries, and by mid-season had lost his job
to Garo Yepremian, a 150-pound, left-footed,
soccer-style kicker from the Mediterranean
island of Cyprus. Some writers thought that Garo,
with his scrawny physique and unorthodox kicking style, had "psyched" the bigger, stronger,
more experienced Walker. "Naw," said Wayne,
"It wasn't Garo. I was kicking lousy even before
we got him. It was me. I'd just lost all my confidence. I was making juvenile errors like looking
up when I kicked instead of keeping my head
down and my eye on the ball. I knew I could kick,
but it had gotten to be a mental thing with me."

Walker was not bitter at being displaced as
the Lion kicker. Indeed, he was delighted when
Yepremian kicked six field goals to set an NFL
single-game record and defeat the Minneosta
Vikings, 32-21. Yepremian told reporters that
Wayne had given him advice on how to get his
kicks away faster, and had tried to transmit to him
the little things Walker had learned the hard

way as an NFL kicker. "If our positions had been reversed," Yepremian said candidly, "I don't think I would have done as much. I might have been jealous." Garo knew that in setting his record, he had also broken Walker's Lion field goal record of four in one game.

A few days after Yepremian's record-setting game, Walker approached the Detriot public relations director, Lyall Smith. "You going to put an asterisk next to Garo's record?" Wayne asked with a straight face.

"Asterisk?" Smith replied, puzzled.

Walker laughed. "Yeah, an asterisk. I mean, like Roger Maris when he hit sixty-one home runs. You should put an asterisk in there next to Garo's name to indicate the difference—left-footed, Armenian–Cypriote soccer-style kicker instead of right-footed American."

Walker could make jokes, but he knew that his kicking failures were no laughing matter. He felt that he had to do something to untie the mental knot that bound his confidence. Wayne decided to risk the jeers of his teammates and skeptical reporters by consulting a hypnotist—a qualified medical hypnotist, not a quack. "A neighbor told me he had quit smoking through hypnosis," Walker explained, "so I figured maybe the same doctor could help me with my kicking."

The treatment was slow but successful. Before long Walker was drilling the ball between the goal posts from 50 yards out during off season practice sessions. In 1967, he reclaimed at least

During the game, Walker gives some experienced advice to a young teammate, Paul Naumoff.

part of his field goal job from Yepremian. The Lions discovered that Garo was most effective in close, but lost some of his accuracy when asked to kick long-distance field goals. Walker drew that assignment again. In 1968 the Lions tried to settle the problem by drafting a rookie kicker, Jerry DePoyster, who they felt could hit long and short. But it's a comfort to know that Wayne Walker is still available. After all, Wayne is now the second highest scorer in Detroit Lion history with 319 points. Only Doak Walker, the marvelous Lion halfback of the 1950s, has more—534 points.

Surely, Wayne's 319 points will be surpassed someday by another Detroit Lion. But it will be a lot more difficult to surpass the twelve seasons of brilliant linebacking he has already given the Lions. For that matter, few men in the NFL—past or present—have done better than Wayne Walker.

DAVE ROBINSON

The seconds ticked off relentlessly for the Green Bay Packers and the Dallas Cowboys on the last day of 1967. Down in the gully of the Cotton Bowl in Dallas, the divisional champions of the National Football League were playing for the league crown—plus a chance to advance to the Super Bowl with its $23,000-a-man bonanza. With 1:58 minutes to go in the game, Green Bay held the lead, 34-27. But Dallas had possession of the football and was driving steadily toward the Packer goal.

Then came the play that could have decided the game. Cowboy quarterback Don Meredith called for a pass. His intended receiver was end Frank Clarke. The pass was never completed, but it might just as well have been. Field Judge Fritz Graf's whistle shrilled. The official had detected pass interference on the part of Green Bay's left linebacker, Dave Robinson. The Cowboys were given the ball on the Packer 2-yard line, first down and goal to go.

Furiously, Robinson disputed the call. "I wasn't even near the play," he protested. Dave did not have to be told what the penalty had done to his team's chances. There was ample time for the powerful Cowboys to ram across for a touchdown, kick the tying extra point and send the game into a sudden-death overtime period.

Grimly, the Green Bay defense rose up—as it has so many times. Three times the Cowboys tried to score, and three times they failed. Now it was fourth-and-two—last chance for Dallas. The Cowboys called a quarterback option pass, and Don Meredith rolled out toward the right sideline, his arm upraised as if to pass. They key man on the play was Dave Robinson, who had been the culprit a minute before.

Robinson had two responsibilities. His primary assignment was to shoot across the line of scrimmage in order to force Meredith inside, so the Dallas quarterback could not turn the corner and run into the Packer end zone. In addition, Robinson had to jostle the great Cowboy pass receiver, Bob Hayes, in an attempt to keep him from breaking clear.

Robinson quickly carried out his assignment of slowing down Hayes, then rushed Meredith. The 245-pound linebacker descended on the quarterback like a great, sweaty Goliath. With Robinson wrapped around him, Meredith was unable to throw an accurate pass. Finally, he got rid of the ball, but Green Bay defensive back Tom Brown intercepted the pass in the end zone for the game-saving touchback. Dave Robinson the goat had become Dave Robinson the hero.

Actually, Dave was not fully satisfied with the clutch play he had made to stop Meredith. He felt that he had been late in reaching the Dallas quarterback and that, in grabbing Meredith by his left arm, he had permitted Don to unload one last pass with his free right arm.

The 1969 season marked the 28-year-old Dave Robinson's seventh year in professional football. A strong-side linebacker, he had proved himself to be the best in the business at his position. For four straight years he was named All-Pro.

Robinson is an immovable object against whom the strongest NFL runners shatter. He is also an irresistible force, able to squeeze ruinous mistakes out of the most knowledgeable quarterbacks in the NFL. "Trying to pass over Robinson," former San Francisco Forty-Niner Coach Jack Christiansen once said, "is like trying to pass over the Empire State Building."

Robinson has been an overwhelmingly consistent performer for Green Bay, under both Vince Lombardi and Phil Bengtson, but Dave is primarily remembered for his superb defensive plays under pressure.

One occurred in 1965 when the Packers were battling the Baltimore Colts for the Western Division title. Green Bay held a 14-13 lead, but Baltimore drove down to the Packer 2 yard line with only a minute remaining in the first half. Baltimore quarterback Gary Cuozzo decided to risk a pass, since he expected the Green Bay defense to pinch in tight. Cuozzo's call was for a short pass to fullback Jerry Hill, floating out in the right flat.

Robinson was expecting the Colts to run with the football. But when he saw that the Colts' tight end, John Mackey, wasn't trying to block him hard the way he usually did, Dave realized that the Colts were going to pass. He later described the play: "I went with Hill, and Cuozzo tried to drop the football over my head."

Cuozzo, under fierce pressure from the Packers' onrushing left end, Willie Davis, miscalculated slightly. He threw the ball too low. Robinson picked it out of the air and huff-puffed 87 yards to the Colt 10-yard line, where he was tackled. The Packers scored on the next play and took a 21-13 lead into the dressing room at halftime. "It was a fourteen-point play," Packer Coach Vince Lombardi said later, "and the turning point of the game." Baltimore never recovered from the shock and Green Bay went on to win, 42-27.

In 1966, Robinson short-circuited the Colts again. This time Green Bay was attempting to nurse a 14-10 lead through the last minute of play. But Baltimore's great quarterback, John Unitas, was beginning to drive his team downfield. With the ball on the Packer 23, Unitas dropped back to pass on the muddy grass, but his receivers were covered. Resolutely, Unitas started to run with the ball, heading straight down the middle of the field. He never saw mammoth Willie

Two All-Pros, Cleveland's Leroy Kelly and Green Bay's Robinson, try to outfox each other.

Davis thunder up from behind him. Davis' objective was not simply to tackle Unitas—he wanted to tackle the quarterback and cause a fumble. Davis yanked at Unitas' right arm as he hit the Colt from the blind side. The football popped out of Unitas' grasp and dribbled forward to the Packer 9-yard line. There Dave Robinson promptly flopped on the ball and hung on to it for dear life. Green Bay won the game, 14-10.

The record shows that Dave Robinson is a great linebacker. He made All-NFL often. But why is he so good?

"Dave has exceptionally good hands, good speed and he's a good tackler," said Henry Jordan, who for so many years was an All-NFL defensive tackle for Green Bay. "What makes a linebacker successful is being able to analyze the play real quickly and, if it's a run, to fill his hole. If it's a pass, he must be able to go deep. Dave can do all that."

Robinson himself explains the corner linebacking business in more technical detail.

"I think linebacking is the most difficult job on the football field," he said. "When you say a quarterback is out to fool a defense, what you mean is that he is out to fool the linebackers. The quarterback knows what the front four will do—rush. And he doesn't have time to fool the deep backs. He's out to make three linebackers think one thing—pass! He gives the ball to a back and

Dave charges fearlessly against a Detroit kicker.

the back has running room. Or he's out to make
you think—run! You rush up and the pass receivers go by you. A lineman worries about
stopping runs. A deep back worries about stopping
passes. A linebacker's got to worry about stopping
runs *and* passes.

"But we help each other. I help the deep backs
on a pass and they'll help me on a run. Like Herb
Adderley may say to me: 'Don't worry about the
tight end cutting you down on this play. You
play him for a pass and if he cuts you down I'll
come up to stop the run.' But you got to read the
play. You got to read keys. And read them quick
—no more than two seconds. You take more than
two seconds, you're dead, because that quarterback can throw in three seconds. You see a guard
pull, a back come at you—those are keys. You got
to decide right then—is it a pass or a run? The
keys are real and they are right now." At this
juncture the beast in Dave Robinson bobbed to
the surface. Forearms flailing to fend off imaginary blockers, he plowed toward the root of the
play. "Down there," Robinson continued, "it
is a blood bath. Someone's always out to stick a
linebacker."

To almost all opponents, Robinson is considered
the strongest left linebacker in the game. But he
actually varies his weight according to the team
he is playing against. "I like to play heavy, about
245 pounds, against a team like Detroit and
lighter against other clubs. But if I drop below
235, I'm too weak to handle people."

It is difficult to imagine the prospect of Robinson's being too weak to handle anybody. Actually, body contact is his specialty. "I respect the player who hits me the hardest and who can also take my best shot," Dave once said. "Take John Mackey of the Colts. We're good friends, but we really go at it. I never want John to leave the field saying, 'I think Dave has lost something.'"

But Dave Robinson cannot be marked as a purely physical bull of a man. He has a civil engineering degree from Penn State. He has also played in bridge tournaments and acquired an expertise in chess. In his free time, he reads books on philosophy and politics. There is a sharp mind controlling all that muscle.

Born in Mt. Holly, New Jersey, on May 3, 1941, Robinson grew up in a family of eight children. While he was a freshman in high school, his father died. To help support the family, Dave took a part-time job as a garbage collector. Dave still found time to develop in sports. In fact, he became one of the finest athletes ever to attend Moorestown High School. He played basketball for a varsity team that won forty-four games in succession. He played baseball and hit .425 his senior year. But it was in football—as a tackle—that he really starred for Moorestown.

When he played college football at Penn State, Robinson was the most versatile man on the team. Basically, he was an end. But he was a tight end who blocked so well and so often that his presence was like having an extra offensive tackle in the lineup. He was also a reliable pass receiver with good, sure hands. On defense, Dave was Penn State's best player, leading the team in tackles. He played more minutes than anybody else on the squad. In 1962, his senior year, he made the All-America team.

Rival college coaches learned to steer their offenses away from Dave. When Army played Penn State, West Point Coach Paul Dietzel discovered that Robinson was as tough as advertised. "We ran a few plays in his direction," Dietzel recalled, "and then stayed away from him. I thought he might swallow my quarterback."

Green Bay made Robinson its first-round draft pick for the 1963 season. But for the first time in years Dave had a difficult time adjusting. His main problem was that the Packers decided he was too small at 238 pounds to play defensive end. Instead, Coach Vince Lombardi decided to switch Robinson to linebacker, a position Dave knew little about. As a result, he sat restlessly on the bench while veterans Dan Currie, Bill Forester and Ray Nitschke backed up the line. Robinson was despondent then but later, when looking back, he saw how raw he had been. "I was like a newborn baby when I came to the Packers," he said. "I knew nothing."

Fortunately, Dave found a good instructor in

After an interception, Robinson looks like a tight end roaring down the field. He once played the flank.

the experienced right linebacker, Forester, who was playing his last season with the Packers. "Everything else I've learned is a refinement of what Bill taught me about linebacking," Robinson said.

One of the things Dave had to learn was the art of knowing when to drop back to defend against a pass and when to remain where he was to meet a running play. "I'd read pass on almost every play," he recalled. "I ran back every time the quarterback showed me pass-action (a fake hand-off to a running back). There were always acres of grass in front of me."

Robinson played a little starting football late in 1963. When Ray Nitschke was injured in the Thanksgiving Day game against the Lions, Bill Forester took over as middle linebacker and Robinson started at right linebacker. He played well enough to earn the regular job in 1964, after Forester had departed, and held it until he suffered a crippling knee injury in mid-season. Then, as he was undergoing the physical problems that eventually led to an off-season knee operation, Robinson had to watch glumly as Lee Roy Caffey, whom the Packers had obtained from the Philadelphia Eagles, moved ahead of him at weak-side linebacker.

But the Packers had no intention of letting Robinson waste away on the bench. Green Bay traded the aging Dan Currie to the Los Angeles Rams and switched Robinson to Currie's position at left linebacker. Dave was uncertain at first.

The position was new to him and he was worried that his knee would not hold up. But when it did, his speed, maneuverability and confidence returned. Before long, Dave Robinson at strong-side linebacker had become the best in pro football, maybe the best ever.

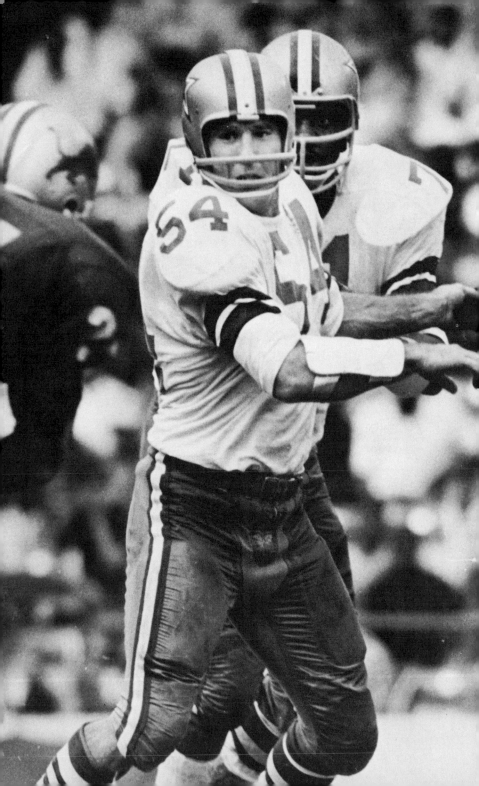

CHUCK HOWLEY

There was no way Chuck Howley could have caught Leroy Kelly. No way. After all, Howley is a 220-pound linebacker for the Dallas Cowboys. Granted, he is a fast linebacker who once ran the hundred in 10.1 seconds, but that was back in West Virginia University, when he played fullback. Kelly, the great Cleveland Brown runner, has done the hundred in 9.8 seconds far more recently than that and is a justifiably famous breakaway back.

Howley and Kelly met in the 1967 Eastern Division championship game, in which Dallas massacred Cleveland, 52-14. On one offensive sequence, the Browns ran Kelly on a strongside sweep and sprang him loose down the sideline behind letter-perfect blocking. Kelly had a 10-yard lead on the nearest Cowboy defender, Chuck Howley. Furthermore, Howley did not have what coaches call "a good tackling angle" on Leroy. It had to be a foot race, pure and simple, between the two pro stars.

As a capacity Cotton Bowl crowd watched disbelievingly, the tortoise (Howley) put on a tremendous burst of speed and caught the hare (Kelly) from behind. Then Howley flattened Kelly with a bone-rattling tackle. Kelly settled for a 46-yard gain when almost everybody had conceded him a touchdown—everybody, that is, but Chuck Howley.

"Chuck just has that great explosion," said the Dallas linebacking coach, Jerry Tubbs, who used to play with Howley. "He explodes like a good back. I honestly think he could have been an offensive back in this league."

Fast enough to be fullback, Howley makes a formidable left linebacker. In the language of the pros, the left linebacker is the "strong-side" linebacker; that is, he plays the side toward which the offense usually stations both its flanker and its tight end. Thus the strong-side linebacker has greater pass coverage duties than the weak-side, or right linebacker. What's more, the strong-side linebacker must also be ready for running plays; almost 80 per cent of any team's ground attack is directed toward the strong side, since that's where the heaviest blocking power lies.

Howley and Dave Robinson of the Packers are the top strong-side linebackers in the National Football League. Each gets the job done in his own way. Robinson is bigger and stronger. Howley is faster and more experienced. At one point in 1968, Howley actually was tied for the NFL lead in pass interceptions. Chuck also got extremely high ratings for his ability to sense what play is coming.

"It's just something I've developed over the years," Howley said matter-of-factly. "You just

notice certain keys to a play. Like on the draw
play, you watch the position of the back's arms.
If his arms come up, you know he's going to take
the ball." Of course, on some play-action plays
—plays on which the quarterback fakes a hand-off
to a runner to hold the linebackers in place while
he fades to pass—there are no "keys" to read.
Nevertheless, Howley almost invariably guesses
correctly—which is what makes a great linebacker.

Chuck insists that much of his success stems
from the fact that he plays with an outstanding
defensive unit. The Cowboy front four—the so-
called "Doomsday Defense"—rushes enemy
passes ferociously and does just as good a job shut-
ting off the rushing game. Cowboy coach Tom
Landry is the man who perfected the 4-3 defense,
and he remains its finest practitioner. Even so,
Dallas occasionally goes into the five-back defensive alignment—the "Dooley defense" developed
by Coach Jim Dooley of the Chicago Bears and
used on obvious passing downs.

In 1968, against the Detroit Lions and their
rookie quarterback, Greg Landry, Howley turned
the five-back defense to his own advantage. When
Dallas inserts a fifth defensive back, Howley's
job is to cover the opposing tight end. On this
play against Detroit, Chuck guessed that the tight
end would execute a pattern which would take
him to the sideline. But the Lion end did not run
a sideline route. He just kept on going straight
ahead while quarterback Landry, in his inex-

perience, attempted to force a long sideline pass
to his split end, who was tightly guarded by another Dallas defender.

Since Howley was already out there on the
sideline, he figured that his teammate might
need some help. Howley joined him in covering
the Lion split end, intercepted Landry's pass and
rumbled 35 yards for a touchdown that gave Dallas an insurmountable halftime lead.

It was a crucial play. But the Cowboys have become used to Chuck's presence in the right place
at the right time. In 1967, for example, quarterback Frank Ryan of the Cleveland Browns tried
to pass from deep in his own territory. Ryan
had, for once, outguessed Howley. With Chuck
out of position, Ryan attempted to loft the ball
over the linebacker's head. Had the pass been
completed, a long gain might have resulted—and
since the second half had just begun, the Browns
might have gathered the momentum necessary to
beat Dallas.

So there was Chuck Howley, trapped at the
line of scrimmage, with the football spiralling
over his head. Desperately, Chuck backpedaled,
back, back, back. At the last possible moment, he
leaped high and deflected the football, tapping
it into the air and away from the would-be Cleveland receiver. But that wasn't the end of the play.
Somehow, Howley regained his equilibrium in

*Chuck Howley hits an opponent low and teammate Le-
Roy Jordan hits him high—the way tackles are supposed
to be made.*

a flash, caught the football before it hit the ground, and ran 28 yards for a touchdown. Frank Ryan had a chance to tackle him at the goal line, but Howley just faked him out like a swivel-hipped halfback.

As Howley left the field with the rest of the defensive platoon, Cowboy offensive halfback Dan Reeves came up and said jokingly, "Watch that stuff, Howley."

Chuck laughed. "Whaddya mean, *Howley?* My name is Gale Sayers." Chuck's play proved crucial as the Cowboys won, 21-14.

Actually, Howley shocks even his teammates with the way he can run. They still talk about the way he overtook Leroy Kelly, but that was because it happened in such an important game. There are other memorable Howley plays, too. In 1965 Cowboy safetyman Mel Renfro, who has the kind of speed that almost got him into the Olympics, intercepted a pass and ran 90 yards for a touchdown. The man who stayed out in front of Renfro and obliterated the last St. Louis Cardinal tackler was none other than Chuck Howley. And in 1966 Howley did the same thing when a Dallas back returned a punt 85 yards for a touchdown against Green Bay. This time the man Howley led downfield was Olympic sprint champion Bob Hayes.

That same year, 1966, Howley did some long-distance running on his own. Against the Atlanta Falcons, he picked up a loose ball on the Dallas 3-yard line, squirmed away from Falcon fullback

Ernie Wheelwright, and steamed 97 yards for a touchdown. His 97-yard run fell only a yard short of the NFL record of 98 yards set by, of all people, George Halas of the Chicago Bears on November 4, 1923. On that memorable occasion, Halas caught a Jim Thorpe fumble in mid-air and just managed to outrace the great Indian back all the way down the field.

Howley firmly believes that being a linebacker for the Cowboys is more demanding than being a linebacker for the Halas Bears, the team for which he first played when he entered the NFL. "When I was with Chicago," Chuck said, "the linebacker's primary responsibility was the run. Then came the pass. Here at Dallas the primary job is both the run and the pass. We cover more backs than any other team in the league. That's why Coach Landry keeps his linebackers under 230 pounds, at about 225. Any of us can keep up with a back on a pass route for the first thirty yards. If our line hasn't gotten to the quarterback by that time, it's liable to be a touchdown anyway. On the longer pass routes, you can tell by the back's momentum as he comes at you whether he's going deep or not."

The Bears, Howley explained, got away with putting linebacker pass defense second because Bear linebackers were soon taught the indelicate art of annihilating receivers before they ever got in position to catch the ball. "We'd knock down the tight end or the flanker and then drift into the flat to cover a pass out there," Chuck said in describing his days as a Bear linebacker. "That was all."

Because of his anticipation and quickness, Howley is best known as a pass-intercepting linebacker, but among opponents he is also feared for this ability to "chuck" ends and backs as they head downfield on pass plays. What is "chucking?" It is better illustrated than described.

In 1967, the Cowboys were playing the New Orleans Saints and Howley was stationed at his customary left-linebacker spot. Bill Kilmer, the Saints' quarterback, took the snap from center and started to roll out toward Howley's side of the field. As Kilmer gathered speed, the New Orleans fullback, Jim Taylor, the former Green Bay Packer famed for his toughness, slid out as a potential pass receiver. But Howley would not let Taylor get by. He "chucked" Jimmy with a headache-inducing slam on the back of Taylor's helmet and knocked the New Orleans star flat on his face—all this with one brawny arm.

While flattening Taylor, Howley kept his eyes riveted on Kilmer. Howley waited to see if the quarterback meant to pass or run with the ball, all the while closing in steadily on Kilmer, compelling him to make up his mind rapidly. Finally, Kilmer cocked his arm to pass as he saw Jim Taylor get back to his feet at the spot Howley had "chucked" him. But the young Saint passer had

Unusually speedy for a big man, Chuck pursues Green Bay's Elijah Pitts.

waited too long. By this time Howley was on top of him. The Dallas linebacker hit Kilmer just as he tried to recall his pass and tuck the football back into his mid-section. Too late! The ball squirted high into the air and Howley gobbled it up for another interception.

Charles Louis Howley has always been a fine all-round athlete. As a high school boy in Wheeling, West Virginia, he was an All-State fullback. Then, when he went on to the University of West Virginia, he won varsity letters in five sports: football, track, swimming, wrestling and gymnastics. Chuck won the Southern Conference one-meter diving championship and, although he weighed 215 pounds, ran the 100- and 220-yard dashes for the Mountaineer track team, as well as putting the shot and throwing the javelin. Howley would have played on the baseball team, too. He had the ability, but the baseball season conflicted with spring football practice, and football has always been Howley's favorite sport.

In his sophomore year at West Virginia, Chuck played middle guard in the defensive line. He was flanked by two seniors who went on to become outstanding professionals—Sam Huff with the New York Giants and later the Washington Redskins, and Bruce Bosley of the San Francisco Forty-Niners. Both Huff and Bosley played defensive tackle at West Virginia. Despite the presence of Huff and Bosley, Howley made the All-Conference team as a sophomore. He repeated the honor in his junior and senior seasons. As a senior, he was the Southern Conference's Player of the Year and made some All-America teams.

One of Chuck's coaches at West Virginia was Bob Snyder, the backup quarterback to Sid Luckman when both were with the Chicago Bears back in the 1940s. Snyder called Howley "the finest pro linebacker prospect I've ever coached," so it was hardly an accident that the Bears drafted Chuck on the first round—and hardly surprising that Howley became a first-stringer for Chicago in 1958, his rookie season.

In 1959, however, Howley injured his knee and was able to play only three games. He underwent surgery and felt he had recovered sufficiently to reclaim his job with Chicago, but the Bears thought otherwise. After four games of the 1960 season, the Bears placed Howley on the injured reserve list. Chuck went home to Wheeling, and went into the gasoline station business. He did not play football in 1960.

Just when Howley thought his football days were over, the Bears traded him to Dallas for a second-round draft choice. Abruptly, Chuck decided to un-retire.

"When I got to Dallas in 1961," he recalled, "I asked if I should tape the knee that had given me trouble. The doctor said no, not unless I wanted to. I wasn't too conscious of it so it's never given me any more trouble."

But Howley has given trouble to every offense that comes up against him. Perhaps his greatest

*Chuck, driving low and hard, prepares
to roar through Washington's line.*

single season came in 1965, when he made All-NFL. He played the last three games despite a painful leg injury because he had his heart set on making the Pro Bowl squad for the first time. Chuck made the team and his one-handed interception of a John Brodie pass made a sizable contribution toward the East team's victory.

At age 34 Howley has established himself as one of the NFL's quality linebackers. He was named to the All-NFL team again in 1969. Retirement is the last thing on his mind. Redemption is the first thing. The Cowboys were expected to reach the NFL championship round, and possibly the Super Bowl in both 1968 and 1969. But instead they were defeated soundly by the Cleveland Browns in the Eastern play-offs both times.

"I feel greater now than I have in the last two or three years," Howley said. "I feel young, quicker and faster. Maybe that's because I've gotten my weight down to 220 pounds, and I feel my agility is much greater now. Of course, whether I'm as strong against running plays, I don't know. One thing may have to suffer for the other. But for some reason I just didn't get tired last year. People—writers and everybody—keep telling me I'm older. I keep telling them I don't agree. They say I'm losing speed and I just try to show them I'm not. I think I'm just getting my second wind."

MIKE CURTIS

The Baltimore Colts are one of several pro teams which subscribe to a college scouting pool with the cryptic initials CEPO. Along with such teams as the Green Bay Packers, the New York Giants, and the Cleveland Browns, the Colts receive computerized scouting reports on virtually every college football player given a chance to succeed in the pros.

In 1964, the Colts won the National Football League's Western Division championship, then lost the league title to the Browns, 27-0. As a result, the Colts decided to go after a top linebacker in the college draft. CEPO reports told the Baltimore front office that two outstanding collegiate linebackers would be available. The kingpin, Dick Butkus of Illinois, was beyond the Colts' reach —since Baltimore would be the next-to-last team to make its selection. Sure enough, Butkus was snatched up almost immediately by the Chicago Bears. So Baltimore "settled" for the second linebacker on the CEPO list—comparatively unknown Mike Curtis, of Duke University. Whatever fame the 226-pound Curtis had achieved in college, he had achieved playing fullback on offense. In his senior year a severe shoulder dislocation had handicapped him, although he still gained 497 yards on 124 carries and established a Duke career rushing record.

But the Colts liked what the scouts said about Curtis' linebacking ability.

"Will be an outstanding outside linebacker in the pros," reported Peahead Walker of the Giants. "A fierce tackler with fine pursuit. A very fine football player."

"I like his quickness," wrote Pat Peppler of the Packers. "He hits."

After five seasons with the pros, Mike Curtis has vindicated the judgment of the Colts—and the CEPO scouts. Once he was given a chance to play regularly, he quickly developed into one of the best left corner linebackers in the league. And in 1969, when the Colts became dissatisfied with their middle linebacking, Mike was moved to this position—and played it well. In all probability, Curtis will continue to be a middle linebacker. He has the speed, agility, strength, aggressiveness and intelligence that the position demands. As a corner linebacker, Curtis was almost on a par with the incomparable Dave Robinson of Green Bay. As a middle linebacker, Mike may someday be on a par with the great Tommy Nobis of the Atlanta Falcons, or Dick Butkus of the Bears. The fact that Baltimore has moved to the American Conference—out of the same division as Butkus and Nobis—may even speed up his hopes for All-Star stature.

According to Baltimore assistant coach Dick

Curtis corrals Ram quarterback Roman Gabriel.

Bielski, Curtis is as quick, as strong and as fast as any linebacker who ever played the game. "He just can't stand to be blocked," Bielski said.

Mike himself has admitted that something comes over him when he steps onto a football field. He once said, "Off the field I'm a gentleman. But when I'm on the field I'm an animal. I don't know what makes me so aggressive. I guess it's just that I like to be *complete*. I don't like to be beaten. I enjoy contact a lot. I like to hit somebody. Some people say I didn't have this reputation for aggressiveness when I was at Duke. But it was there. I didn't talk much with sports writers when I was in college, so they didn't really know what I was like, I guess."

Like Ray Nitschke of the Green Bay Packers, Curtis does not like writers to exaggerate his super-aggressive nature, making him seem like "a crazy nut." He points out that the Colts knew he was a hard-nose when they drafted him. "That's why they wanted me," he said. "I led my college team in making tackles."

Don Shula, then the Colt coach, agreed. "Curtis was one of the main differences between the Colt championship team of 1968 and the one we had in 1967. He worked his way into the starting lineup and did a great job. He's as fast as a back, which he was in college, has fantastic quickness, a mean streak, and is intelligent."

But when columnists write about Curtis, it is the "mean streak" that attracts their attention. It makes much better copy than Mike's shrewdness.

After watching the Colts destroy the Los Angeles Rams, 27-10, in a climactic 1968 NFL game, Larry Merchant of the New York *Post* wrote:

"Mike Curtis, a linebacker for the Baltimore Colts, was a history major at Duke. After yesterday's performance against the Los Angeles Rams, it was obvious who his favorite people in history are—Genghis Khan, William the Conqueror, Sitting Bull, Bonnie and Clyde, and Vince Lombardi."

Two plays in particular left a lasting impression on Merchant. What those plays did to the Rams will be obvious. On the first, the Rams tried an end run around Curtis' side. Mike reacted savagely. He smashed into the Ram blocker with his shoulder, and the man went down as though he had been shot. That left the Los Angeles ball carrier, Dick Bass, naked to his enemy. Curtis did not bother with a tackle. He nearly beheaded poor Bass with one muscular forearm.

Later in the game, the Colts threw a blitz at the Rams' tall quarterback, Roman Gabriel. Curtis shot the gap like a stone propelled by David's slingshot. He got to Gabriel before the quarterback could set up. Curtis delivered a crunching neck tackle. "He jarred the ball loose from Gabriel," reported Merchant. "For a moment you weren't sure if it was the ball or Gabriel's head rolling around."

Curtis was coy about his ferocity. "I just hide behind my defensive end, Bubba Smith, who is 6-feet 7-inches tall and weighs 290 pounds, and get them when they're not looking," Mike explained. But his Colt teammates laugh when Curtis talks like that. They know that he hides behind no one. As a matter of fact, in a 1968 game Bubba Smith made three consecutive tackles and forced the opposition to punt. As the Colt defense came to the sidelines, Curtis hurled his helmet to the ground in frustrated fury because he had not been able to get into the action. "I was glad Bubba made the tackles," Mike said, "but I get awfully emotional by the time a game starts. I want the Colts and myself to be the best in the world. I despise being second in anything."

Curtis can be as rough on his fellow Colts in practices as he is on NFL rivals in games. "Sometimes he just loses control," said teammate Bill Curry, an offensive center. Curry and Curtis are roommates, too, though on the practice field they attack each other like cat and dog. Their flurries of anger soon blow over, though. "It's like arguing with your wife," Curtis explained. "Bill and I always make up."

One of Mike's battles with a teammate got him into trouble in 1968. During a practice session, Curtis' temper rose and he leveled rookie fullback Terry Cole without warning. The two players had never had a run-in before. The offense was so blatant that Coach Shula banished Curtis to the sidelines for an hour. The incident took place during the week of an important game with the Los Angeles Rams, a game that would determine first place in the rugged Coastal Division.

"I was fired up and nervous," Mike said later. "Something just clicked. I deserved what coach gave me." Said the awed rookie Cole, when he got over the shock: "I'm just glad Mike's on my side."

Yet there is another side to Curtis. When he demolished Dick Bass, in the game with the Rams, Mike was the first man to call for a stretcher. After the game, Baltimore flanker Jimmy Orr dressed rapidly in front of the locker next to Mike's. "I usually get out of here in a hurry," Orr said, kidding for Curtis' benefit, "so he doesn't hit me."

Since the desire to succeed burns with such intensity inside Mike Curtis, the Colts' stunning defeat by the New York Jets in the Super Bowl came as a staggering blow. Before the game, it was expected that Baltimore would try to break up the Jets' fine passing game by letting Curtis blitz often, from the strong side behind Bubba Smith's powerful rush. Sadly for Baltimore, the strategy did not work. Jet quarterback Joe Namath found that he could gain against the right side of the Colt defense, so he directed his fire in that direction. Jet tackle Dave Herman, a converted guard, kept Bubba Smith away from Namath with surprising regularity. And the New York backs, all excellent blockers, picked up Curtis and other Colts when they did come blitzing through. In many respects, the Super Bowl passed Curtis by—to his chagrin.

Since Mike Curtis comes from nearby Rock-

ville, Maryland, where he was an outstanding player at Richard Montgomery High School, his success with the Colts is a case of a local boy making good in front of his friends and family. He was delighted when the Colts drafted him. But the delight tapered off in his rookie year when he found himself listed as Baltimore's third-string fullback. (Even as a linebacker today, Curtis still wears a fullback's number, 32, on his jersey.)

Mike's problem was simple. The Colts had acquired a promising middle linebacker, Dennis Gaubatz, during an off-season trade, and the team already had three top-notch linebackers—Don Shinnick, Jackie Burkett and Steve Stonebreaker —for the two outside positions. So Curtis was used—or, more accurately, not used—in the offensive backfield behind veteran Jerry Hill and Tony Lorick.

In 1966, Mike reported to training camp ten pounds lighter—at 220—believing that less weight would mean more speed and more chance to step ahead as the Baltimore fullback. But, to his surprise, he was assigned to the linebacking unit, and once again found himself playing behind Burkett and Stonebreaker. No one will ever know how long Curtis might have sat on the bench had not both Burkett and Stonebreaker been injured early in the season. Curtis was installed as Baltimore's regular left linebacker.

The 1969 Super Bowl wasn't much fun for Mike, but he did get this one shot at the Jets' Joe Namath.

A few times he nearly trampled the Colt safety-man, Jerry Logan, while pursuing opposing ball-carriers. "I guess you could say my forte was making mistakes aggressively," Curtis confessed. "These things happened because I was in the wrong place and had to do something to atone for not being where I was supposed to be. I'm still learning about defense, and sometimes I think it will take me fifteen years to learn it all."

Despite his overeagerness, Curtis was making an impression on his coaches. "I think he probably is the fastest linebacker in our league," said linebacking coach Chuck Noll, the head coach of the Pittsburgh Steelers. When the Colts timed their players in 1967, the 226-pound Curtis ran the 40-yard dash in 4.7 seconds, which is fast time for a halfback, much less a linebacker. In the run to test agility, only ends Jimmy Orr and Ray Perkins and halfback Lenny Moore did better than Curtis. "Mike has an instinct for the ball that can't be taught," Noll said. "He'll keep improving as he plays and gathers experience."

Despite his mistakes, Curtis did not really hurt the Colts as an inexperienced linebacker in 1966. In his first game as a starter, he led the team in tackles as Baltimore whipped the Detroit Lions, 45-14. He was awarded the game ball. "I really can't get over it," Curtis said proudly. "I was really surprised the fellows gave me the ball. You

Curtis enjoys the fruits of victory with assistant coach John Sandusky.

know, I've never played more than a half-game, and that was in pre-season. I wouldn't have been playing today if Jackie Burkett hadn't been hurt. But I really felt like playing today. I was in the Bear game some last week, and I was really embarrassed because I played so bad."

Curtis was learning that pro defense is even more complex than pro offense. On each offensive play, the attacking team has so many alternatives. In college Curtis had played both ways, and the Duke defense was not complicated. He was virtually on his own. But in the pros, he had trouble figuring out off-tackle plays and sweeps, and when to close the strong-side, or tight end, gap. But his teammates guided him and he improved.

Mike's success in 1966 bolstered his confidence. He felt that 1967 would be even better. It wasn't. In the Colts' third game of the year, against the Forty-Niners, Mike injured his knee and had to undergo surgery. Some players are soon as good as ever after knee surgery. Many never are. They lose one precious step of speed and sink from good to average.

But Curtis came back from his knee operation in 1968 as if he had never been away. He proved in training camp that he had not lost any speed and that he was as pugnacious as ever. In an exhibition game against the AFL Miami Dolphins, Curtis greeted one end sweep by knocking a Dolphin blocker back into a Dolphin ball carrier so hard that both Miami players had to be assisted off the field. Mike insisted, though, that his knee injury had taught him a philosophy of moderation. "The injury gave me a lot of time to think," Curtis said. "I realized that I have to get myself under control if I'm going to have a career in pro football. The Kamikaze stuff is great. That's the way I like to play all the time. But I have to realize that muscle and bone just won't take that completely all-out stuff all the time. You can be putting out maximum effort, but still have yourself under control." It was not just the knee operation that made Curtis wonder about the way he spent his energies. At various stages of his football career—high school, college and pro—he had had a dislocated shoulder, cracked ribs, injured ankles, and broken hands. In addition, both knees have been hurt.

Despite his promises to himself to play more cautiously, Mike Curtis found it hard to change. He had become a star by playing with abandon, and he probably will always play that way. Mike accepts his fate. "I guess I'm branded," he said. "I guess I'm like the old Western gunslinger. Everybody wants a crack at me because I'm supposed to be mean and tough."

Mike Curtis laughed. "You know what would really be a great kick?" he said. "To go up to the next writer who asks me if I'm really an 'animal' and take a bite out of his arm!"

TOMMY NOBIS

Tommy Nobis stands 6-feet 2-inches tall and weighs 242 pounds. He is a red-headed, freckle-faced, bow-legged middle linebacker out of Texas —strong as a steer, tough as a lariat. During Nobis' rookie season with the NFL back in 1966, the Philadelphia Eagles decided to test this $250,000 bonus rookie who was playing with the Atlanta Falcons. They ran an elementary running play, with halfback Timmy Brown carrying on a sweep around the right side.

Nobis sensed what was coming. Just as he had been carefully taught in college and in pro training camp, he executed a dainty little step out to the right, his eyes riveted on Timmy Brown. But Nobis never saw the building that fell on him— 285-pound offensive tackle, Bob Brown.

Brown hit Tommy with the block to end all blocks. "Felt like the world turned upside-down," Nobis recalled later. "All I could see was the sky. Man, I'd never been hit like that."

As for Brown, the crafty tackle admitted that the Eagles had carefully planned the maneuver. "We decided to give the young man a baptism," he said.

The Eagles concentrated on Nobis all afternoon.

They double-teamed him. They tried to throw over him. They tried to run around him. But the young Texan refused to back away. Time and again they had to pry his Number 60 off an Eagle ballcarrier. Said tackle Brown after the Eagles had won the game, 23-10: "Listen, that kid is going to be a great one."

The gigantic Philadelphia tackle proved to be quite a prophet. At the end of that 1966 season, Nobis was voted NFL Rookie of the Year by his fellow players, and also by the *Sporting News* and the Pro Football Writers Association.

Tommy has gone on from there. Playing for the Falcons, an expansion team that has never been better than mediocre, he has developed into one of the three best linebackers in the league. In Atlanta, there is no doubt that Nobis is best. In Chicago, the "experts" give Dick Butkus the edge. And in Green Bay, Ray Nitschke is Mr. Middle Linebacker. But the very fact that Nobis can be compared with stars like Butkus and Nitschke after only four seasons in the NFL—four seasons with a loser—says a lot about Tommy.

The comparison between Nobis and Butkus has been particularly heated and controversial. Nitschke, of course, is a veteran player who is much more experienced than either Nobis or Butkus. But Butkus broke into the NFL only a year before Nobis, so that the two great young middle linebackers can be judged on the same level of experience. And so the argument rages, much as it did over Wilt Chamberlain versus Bill

Goal line stands are Tommy Nobis' specialty. Here Tommy, No. 60, stops Minnesota's powerful Bill Brown.

Russell in basketball and Mickey Mantle versus Willie Mays in baseball.

In 1968, *Sport* magazine attempted to solve the dispute by asking five former All-NFL linebackers to pick the best middle linebacker in football. The jury consisted of Chuck Bednarik, a star with the Eagles for fourteen years; Bill George, fourteen seasons with the Chicago Bears; Bill Pellington, twelve years with the Baltimore Colts; Les Richter, nine years with the Los Angeles Rams; and Joe Schmidt, thirteen years as a Detroit Lion middle linebacker.

Not surprisingly, old pro Nitschke won the poll. But some of the comments about Tommy Nobis indicated how good even highly critical old-timers think he is and can be.

"If I had to take one guy right now," said Bednarik, "it would have to be Nobis. I don't know if Atlanta lets him go on every play. But I do know that he is just about everywhere at once."

Joe Schmidt felt that Nobis' speed was his prime asset. "He's probably faster than Butkus or Nitschke," said Schmidt, "and when he gets a little more experience, he'll get an even quicker jump." Not only is Nobis quick on his feet, but he has that extraordinary ability to anticipate where the next play will go, and he has what the pros call "sideline-to-sideline" speed for the short bursts required of a middle linebacker.

Bednarik felt that playing with a losing team has put Nobis at a disadvantage in any comparison with the other great middle linebackers. "If you've got a good front four," Bednarik explained, "you can be twice as effective with much less effort. But to get knocked down and kicked around, to have to fight off two or three blockers with no support, and finally to go 15 or 20 yards downfield to drag down a runner from behind—that's the kind of thing Nobis has to do, and does. When you play with a winner, the public can't help but notice you. But anybody who has to play with what Nobis does, who gets hit as much as he does, yet comes back to make the play, he's got to be the best."

Nobis' trials with a weak team had unexpected side effects. For example, Ray Prochaska, one of the Los Angeles Rams' assistant coaches, insisted that Tommy acquired more finesse in warding off blockers than any other linebacker in the NFL, including Butkus and Nitschke. To Nobis, however, his ability to fend off blockers is a God-given instinct.

"There really isn't much a coach can show you about how to whip a blocker," Nobis has said. "It's just you and him—and whatever habits you've developed over the years for whipping or getting whipped. Some guys like to use their hands on a blocker and some like to use their forearms. I try to use my hands to keep a blocker away from me, because I figure that if he gets close enough for me to give him a forearm, he is already too close to my body."

At the University of Texas, Tommy was famous for the way he tackled runners "right in the goozle"—meaning the ball carrier's chest. He had learned the technique in high school. But as a pro, he had to make adjustments. Nobis is no longer a goozle-hunter, though his tackling technique remains destructively simple.

"If you get to the ball carrier," he once explained, "shoot your head across the front side of him. If you shoot your head to the inside, all you have is one arm to hold him. Fellows like Ken Willard of the Forty-Niners will rip that arm right off your shoulder."

Nobody rips apart Nobis, though. He is so strong that legends about his muscle power have already begun to take shape. One of Tommy's Atlanta teammates, Bill Martin, was in the Army with Nobis. Martin reports that when Tommy had difficulty putting his M-1 rifle back together after disassembling it, he simply bent the weapon with his bare hands until every part popped back into place!

During his first year in the NFL, Nobis averaged twenty-one tackles a game. Perhaps his finest performance came when the Falcons played the Bears. Everybody was waiting to see whether Nobis would outplay his rival, Dick Butkus. Both players were great, but Nobis was something special. The Bears ran forty-six running plays. Tommy had a hand in thirty-four tackles. Twice he red-dogged into the Chicago backfield to dump

A one-man team in the early years of the Atlanta franchise, Nobis tackled hard and often.

quarterback Rudy Bukich for 8-yard losses. Twice he caught Bear backs from behind after they seemed gone for touchdowns.

"This kid is a whole defense by himself—our whole defense, if you want the truth," Falcon Coach Norb Hecker said in Tommy's rookie year. "Put him with that Bear defensive line and you'd see linebacking like you've never seen before."

Nobis was less willing to claim any victory over the formidable Butkus. One artisan respects the other. "Butkus is to a defense what Gale Sayers is to an offense," Tommy said. "He's in on every play, in every game. I've seen films of Butkus where he runs everywhere after that ball or the ball carrier—and gets 'em, too. Nobody does it better."

During his first year or two in the NFL, some experts felt that Nobis, despite his obvious gifts, might not be mean enough to compete with the professional middle linebackers. Nobis, however, soon found that there was a big difference between college football and the NFL. "It's like the difference between ROTC and the army," he explained. "When I came into the league, I had to gain the respect of my opponents. That didn't mean I had to go out and kill somebody. It was all just part of being a rookie. Maybe I was thinking too much, you know, instead of just reacting to plays. When a receiver crossed in front of me, the coaches wanted me to give him a bump. Lots of times I failed to see him or just didn't think about doing it right because I was worried about being in the proper position. At first I thought I was doing my job if I just brought the runner down. Later I began to realize that in pro ball you have to hit people hard enough to make them remember. If I can get them to thinking that they'd just as soon not run my way, it cuts their effectiveness."

Nobis feels that his major weakness in pro ball originally was trying to help out his teammates too much. The opposition would hit back at holes where he was supposed to be. That came from being inexperienced and over-aggressive.

One of the defensive responsibilities Nobis had to learn in a hurry was what to do on passing plays, which constitute at least half of any normal pro offense. "Most pass plays," Nobis said, "you recognize immediately because their offensive line drops straight back. But when they fire that quickie pass at you, it is so much like a running play that it is tough to stop unless you sense it coming. Maybe you spot the tight end fidgeting around a little before the play, and you guess with him. Guessing right, which comes with experience, is what makes a good linebacker."

Tommy Nobis grew up in San Antonio, Texas, where he was born on September 20, 1943. As a boy, it seemed inconceivable that he would someday become one of the fiercest linebackers in professional football. When Tommy attended Emerson Junior High School in San Antonio, he weighed 120 pounds and played quarterback.

Randy Johnson vividly recalls playing defensive halfback and offensive end for Sam Houston Junior High on the day Emerson J.H.S. defeated Sam Houston, 6-2, with a neat touchdown pass. Times change. Today Johnson plays quarterback for Atlanta, while Nobis struggles to knock down would-be touchdown passes.

Like Dick Butkus, who selected his high school for its football program, Nobis elected to attend Jefferson High in San Antonio because he wanted to play for the Jefferson coach, Pat Shannon. To get to Jefferson meant that Nobis had to wake up at 5:30 in the morning and he rarely got home after football practice before 8:00 or 8:30 P.M.

Nobis' days as a quarterback ended when he repeatedly ran into his own backs. But under Shannon's tutelage, he eventually became an All-State linebacker.

Tommy could have gone to either the University of Oklahoma or the University of Texas. He chose Texas because on the day he visited the Oklahoma campus he heard people make some unpatriotic remarks about Texas.

Nobis became the finest linebacker Texas ever had. During his sophomore season, he played offensive guard as well. In 1964, he led the Longhorns to the national championship, including a 21-17 upset victory in the Orange Bowl over Joe Namath's Alabama team. It was Nobis who stopped Namath short of the Texas goal line on fourth-and-one to save the game. As a senior in 1965, Tommy was a unanimous All-America and

At Texas Nobis was ranked the best lineman in the country. He was pretty good at carrying the ball, too, after interceptions.

won the Outland Trophy as college football's top lineman.

In the pro draft, Nobis was selected by the Houston Oilers of the AFL and the brand-new Atlanta Falcons of the NFL. Houston thought it had an edge when astronaut Frank Borman, orbiting around the earth in his Gemini 7 space capsule, radioed to the Manned Space Center in Houston:

"Tell Tommy Nobis to sign with Houston."

But astronaut Borman's out-of-this-world attempt to recruit Nobis for the Oilers was unsuccessful. Several days later, while Borman was still in orbit, he received the sad bulletin:

"Nobis has signed with Atlanta."

"There's no joy in Mudville," Borman replied glumly.

There was joy in Atlanta, however. The joy increased when Nobis proved in 1966 that he could not only play middle linebacker in the NFL, but play it well. He made the Pro Bowl squad as a rookie. He has, as a matter of fact, made the Pro Bowl every year since—except for 1969, when he was out most of the year with an injured right knee that eventually required surgery.

Nobis was named defensive captain of the Falcons in 1967 and again in 1968 and 1969. But the team's losing record has hurt his pride. He knows that the defeats are not his fault, but every loss stings him badly. "Losing every week," he said, bitterly, "just takes the flavor out of being alive."

But help is on the way for the Falcons. The team had its best season ever in 1969, winning six of fourteen games even though Nobis and the team's top quarterbacks were hurt. More victories seem inevitable when Nobis recovers from his knee operation and the Atlanta franchise ages a bit. Then he won't be losing so often—and life on the gridiron will look a little brighter to him.

INDEX

Page numbers in italics refer to photographs